THE
PARTY
HANDBOOK

Grandma
Rose

David

Penny

Daniel

Becky

Sam

Albert

Jasmine

Lily

Grandad
West

Daisy

Brian

Christi...

THE ROYD FAMILY   **THE KNOTTS FAMILY**   **THE RIDIN...**

THE PARTY HANDBOOK
BY
MALCOLM BIRD & ALAN DART

PAVILION

...mily Tim Edward Jo Saffron James Lucy Harry

...AMILY   THE WALSDEN FAMILY   THE HEBDEN-BRIDGE FAMILY

First published in Great Britain in 1990 by
Pavilion Books Limited
196 Shaftesbury Avenue, London WC2H 8JL

Illustrations and text copyright © Malcolm Bird and Alan Dart 1990

ISBN 1 85145 445 4

Printed and Bound in Singapore by Toppan Printing Company

C6 03999699

IK/5793·4

FOR JOEL, WITH LOVE FROM
HIS GODFATHERS

With thanks to Pamela Todd,
the perfect combination of wonderful agent and dear friend.

CONTENTS

CHAPTER 1

Party Basics

Decorations

Invitations

Always buy your envelopes first, then you can make the invitations to fit. Important details to include are: the name of the party giver and the theme, the date and time, and your address and telephone number. Send out your invitations at least 2 weeks before the party, and keep a list of invited guests to check against as they reply.

Garland

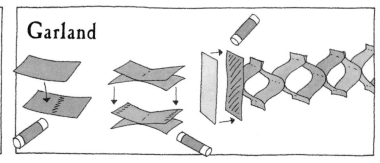

A simple garland can be made from rectangles of coloured tissue paper, measuring twice as long as they are wide. Using a paste stick, glue the pieces together in pairs down the centre line, then glue all the completed pairs together down both sides, and glue a piece of stiff card to each end. This method is used throughout the book.

Mask

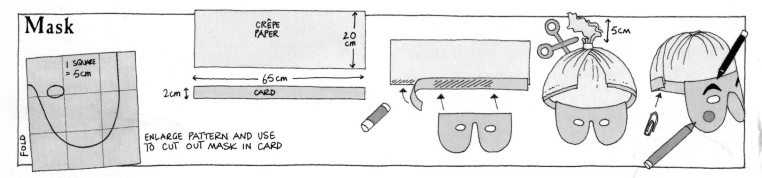

Glue card strip to crêpe paper, then glue mask in centre of strip. Turn inside out, gather edge of crêpe paper and bind with sticky tape, 5cm in from edge. Trim away excess and turn to right side. Adjust to fit head and secure with a paper clip. Create your own characters with paint and pens, or copy the ideas in the following chapters.

Fancy Dress

On this page are the basic patterns used throughout the book. Make a collection of old sheets and curtains, which can be transformed with dye, fabric paint and felt tipped pens – along with buttons, braids and lace cut from old clothes. Crêpe paper makes short-lived outfits, and don't worry about the finish, it's the effect that counts!

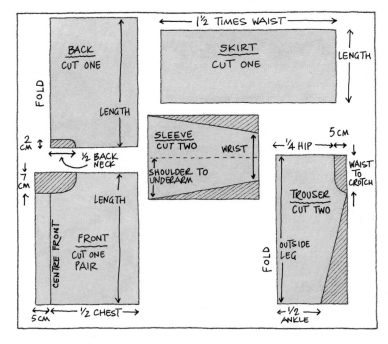

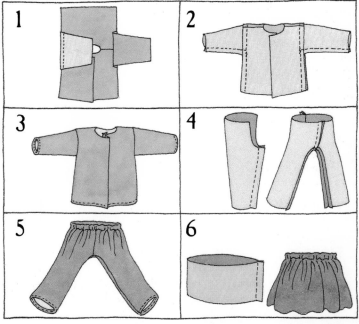

When taking the measurements allow plenty of room for movement, especially at armholes and crutch. Draw the patterns on to strong paper and add 1.5cm all round for seam turnings and hems. Press all seams flat after sewing. If you need to buy fabric, calculate by laying the pattern pieces on the floor within the fabric width.

JACKET: 1. Join shoulders, then sew sleeves to armholes. 2. Sew side and sleeve seams. 3. Turn back 3cm down front edges and press, then hem cuffs and base. Sew collar to neck, or bind. TROUSERS: 4. Sew inside leg seams, then sew crutch seam. 5. Elasticate waist and sew hems. SKIRT: 6. Join side seam, then elasticate waist and sew hem.

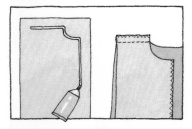

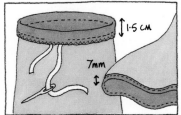

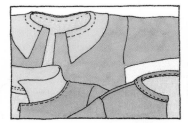

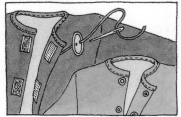

On fabric which frays easily, either outline with fabric glue and cut out when dry (avoid hemming by this method), or work zig zag stitch over cut edge. To elasticate, turn under 1.5cm and sew 5mm from edge, leaving a space open. Thread with 7mm elastic, adjust to fit, and join opening. To hem, turn under 7mm twice and sew down close to edge.

If costume has a collar, sew to neck edge, fold turnings inside garment and work a line of stitching close to fold. Alternatively finish neck by trimming away turning and edging with bias binding. Instead of making awkward buttonholes, sew press studs or pieces of Velcro down the centre front lines of jacket, then sew buttons on top.

Food

You will probably already have your own favourite sandwich fillings and cake recipes, but here are a few more to add to your list. Wherever possible, the main cakes are created from ready-made ingredients, but basic recipes are included for cases where an unusual shape is needed, or where you would prefer something home-made.

Savoury Sandwich Fillings

INTO 250g COTTAGE CHEESE, MIX EITHER —

125g DRAINED CRUSHED PINEAPPLE

OR

75g CHOPPED WALNUTS

OR

2 TABLESPOONS FINELY CHOPPED PEPPERS

MIX 3 MASHED AVOCADOS WITH 1 TABLESPOON EACH OF —

LEMON JUICE

MAYONNAISE

YOU COULD ALSO ADD ½ A CHOPPED CUCUMBER

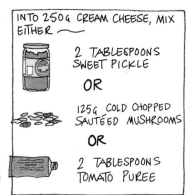

INTO 250g CREAM CHEESE, MIX EITHER —

2 TABLESPOONS SWEET PICKLE

OR

125g COLD CHOPPED SAUTÉED MUSHROOMS

OR

2 TABLESPOONS TOMATO PUREE

MIX 4 MASHED HARD-BOILED EGGS WITH SEASONING AND 1 TABLESPOON MAYONNAISE

YOU COULD ADD 2 TEASPOONS CHOPPED CHIVES TOO!

Sweet Sandwich Fillings

INTO 4 MASHED BANANAS, MIX EITHER —

75g CHOPPED WALNUTS

OR

75g CHOPPED DATES

OR

75g CHOPPED DRIED APRICOTS

INTO 250g CREAM CHEESE, MIX EITHER —

1 TABLESPOON HONEY

OR

125g SWEETENED MASHED BERRIES

OR

1 CHOPPED APPLE OR PEAR

Butter Cream and Glacé Icing

GRADUALLY ADD 225g ICING SUGAR TO 100g BEATEN BUTTER

MIX IN 1 TABLESPOON COLD WATER

ADD BOILING WATER (TAKE CARE!) DROP BY DROP, TO 250g ICING SUGAR...

... UNTIL JUST RUNNY. USE IMMEDIATELY!

Party Cake

CREAM TOGETHER —

175g BUTTER

AND

175g CASTER SUGAR

AND

2 TABLESPOONS HOT WATER

THEN ADD 3 BEATEN EGGS...

...AND FOLD IN 175g SELF RAISING FLOUR

BAKE FOR 50 MINUTES AT 325°F/170°C/GAS MARK 3 (TEST WITH TOOTHPICK)

Small Cakes and Biscuits

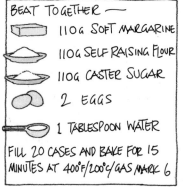

BEAT TOGETHER —

110g SOFT MARGARINE

110g SELF RAISING FLOUR

110g CASTER SUGAR

2 EGGS

1 TABLESPOON WATER

FILL 20 CASES AND BAKE FOR 15 MINUTES AT 400°F/200°C/GAS MARK 6

RUB TOGETHER —

225g PLAIN FLOUR

110g CASTER SUGAR

110g BUTTER

MIX IN —

1 EGG BEATEN WITH 1 TEASPOON WATER

ROLL TO 3MM, CUT OUT AND BAKE FOR 15 MINUTES AT 350°F/180°C/GAS MARK 4

CHAPTER 2

Sweetheart Party

Decorations

Gingerbread Heart and Posy Invitations, and Heart Garland

CUT 2 FELT HEARTS USING CUPID HEART PATTERN (WITH EACH SQUARE = 2CM)

OVERSEW TOGETHER, PADDING LIGHTLY, AND TRIM WITH BRAID, BEAD AND FELT.

SEW LUGGAGE LABEL TO BACK FOR PARTY DETAILS

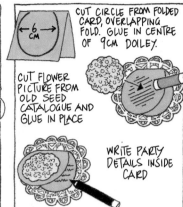

CUT CIRCLE FROM FOLDED CARD, OVERLAPPING FOLD. GLUE IN CENTRE OF 9CM DOILEY.

CUT FLOWER PICTURE FROM OLD SEED CATALOGUE AND GLUE IN PLACE

WRITE PARTY DETAILS INSIDE CARD

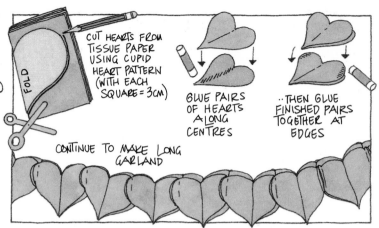

CUT HEARTS FROM TISSUE PAPER USING CUPID HEART PATTERN (WITH EACH SQUARE = 3CM)

GLUE PAIRS OF HEARTS ALONG CENTRES

..THEN GLUE FINISHED PAIRS TOGETHER AT EDGES

CONTINUE TO MAKE LONG GARLAND

Cupid Heart and Valentine Balloons

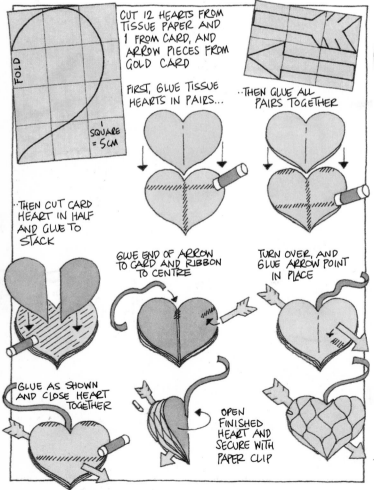

CUT 12 HEARTS FROM TISSUE PAPER AND 1 FROM CARD, AND ARROW PIECES FROM GOLD CARD

FIRST, GLUE TISSUE HEARTS IN PAIRS...

..THEN GLUE ALL PAIRS TOGETHER

1 SQUARE = 5CM

..THEN CUT CARD HEART IN HALF AND GLUE TO STACK

GLUE END OF ARROW TO CARD AND RIBBON TO CENTRE

TURN OVER, AND GLUE ARROW POINT IN PLACE

GLUE AS SHOWN AND CLOSE HEART TOGETHER

OPEN FINISHED HEART AND SECURE WITH PAPER CLIP

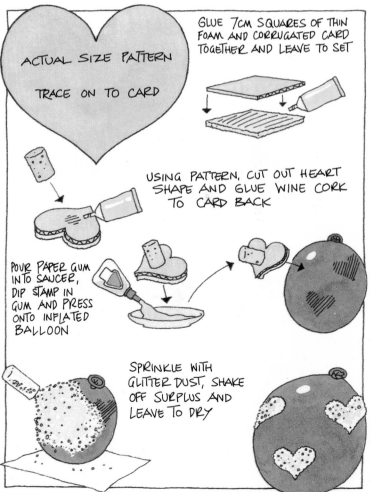

ACTUAL SIZE PATTERN

TRACE ON TO CARD

GLUE 7CM SQUARES OF THIN FOAM AND CORRUGATED CARD TOGETHER AND LEAVE TO SET

USING PATTERN, CUT OUT HEART SHAPE AND GLUE WINE CORK TO CARD BACK

POUR PAPER GUM INTO SAUCER, DIP STAMP IN GUM AND PRESS ONTO INFLATED BALLOON

SPRINKLE WITH GLITTER DUST, SHAKE OFF SURPLUS AND LEAVE TO DRY

Paper Roses and Hands in Heart Wreath

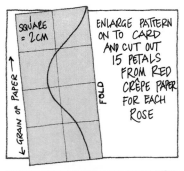

SQUARE = 2CM

GRAIN OF PAPER

FOLD

ENLARGE PATTERN ON TO CARD AND CUT OUT 15 PETALS FROM RED CRÊPE PAPER FOR EACH ROSE

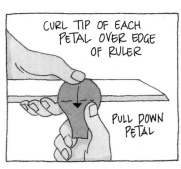

CURL TIP OF EACH PETAL OVER EDGE OF RULER

PULL DOWN PETAL

··THEN CUP EACH PETAL

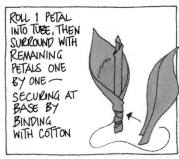

ROLL 1 PETAL INTO TUBE, THEN SURROUND WITH REMAINING PETALS ONE BY ONE — SECURING AT BASE BY BINDING WITH COTTON

WIND NARROW STRIP OF GREEN CRÊPE PAPER ROUND BASE AND GLUE

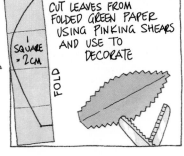

1 SQUARE = 2CM

FOLD

CUT LEAVES FROM FOLDED GREEN PAPER USING PINKING SHEARS AND USE TO DECORATE

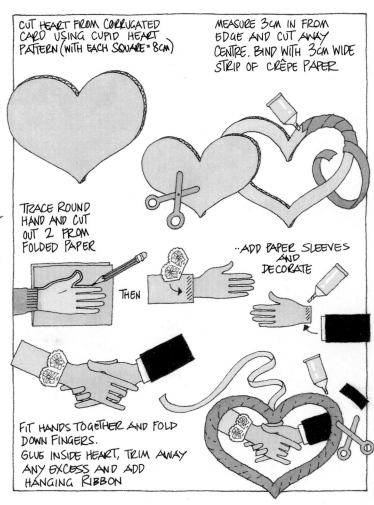

CUT HEART FROM CORRUGATED CARD USING CUPID HEART PATTERN (WITH EACH SQUARE = 8CM)

MEASURE 3CM IN FROM EDGE AND CUT AWAY CENTRE. BIND WITH 3CM WIDE STRIP OF CRÊPE PAPER

TRACE ROUND HAND AND CUT OUT 2 FROM FOLDED PAPER

THEN

··ADD PAPER SLEEVES AND DECORATE

FIT HANDS TOGETHER AND FOLD DOWN FINGERS. GLUE INSIDE HEART, TRIM AWAY ANY EXCESS AND ADD HANGING RIBBON

Confetti Cloth, Lips Straws, Heart Ring, and Posy Plate

SPRINKLE CONFETTI ON PAPER TABLECLOTH AND COVER WITH LAYER OF NET. STICKY TAPE ALL EDGES UNDER TABLE

ADD NET SWAGS AND PAPER ROSES

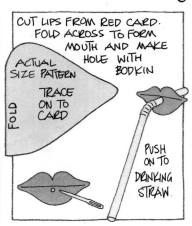

CUT LIPS FROM RED CARD. FOLD ACROSS TO FORM MOUTH AND MAKE HOLE WITH BODKIN

ACTUAL SIZE PATTERN

FOLD

TRACE ON TO CARD

PUSH ON TO DRINKING STRAW.

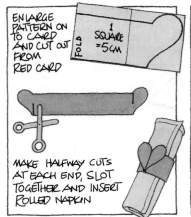

ENLARGE PATTERN ON TO CARD AND CUT OUT FROM RED CARD

1 SQUARE = 5CM

FOLD

MAKE HALFWAY CUTS AT EACH END, SLOT TOGETHER AND INSERT ROLLED NAPKIN

CUT ONE DOILEY IN HALF AND GLUE ROUND EDGE OF PAPER PLATE

GLUE PLATE ON TO ANOTHER DOILEY AND ADD GIFT RIBBON BOW

Fancy Dress

Love Letter

SHOULDER WIDTH

SHOULDER TO WAIST

CUT THESE 2 PIECES FROM CARD

½ SHOULDER TO WAIST

OH, DANIEL THANK YOU!

DRAW STAMP AND WRITE MESSAGE

With love from me to you xx

Lover's Tree

1 SQUARE = 5CM

FOLD

ENLARGE LEAF PATTERN ON TO CARD

BASIC JACKET BACK

5CM

D·R loves E·R

PLACE ON FOLD

BASIC JACKET FRONT

SHOULDER TO ANKLE

Cut a piece of card to fit across shoulders, and down to waist. Measure 5cm in from each end and draw lines to opposite corners. Cut out top triangle. Cut a matching card piece with a pointed top. Join with two 5cm x 15cm fabric strips, and glue tapes to sides. Write message on back and glue piece of paper to inside to curl over head.

Using basic pattern, make a full length jacket in brown fabric, placing centre front line on fold and adding 5cm to centre back line for opening. Fasten with Velcro. Draw heart and initials on front with fabric paint. Using pinking shears, cut leaves from green lining fabric and sew all over a green beret, and to cover jacket sleeves.

Dozen Red Roses

Using chest measurement, cut a square of white bonded interfacing. Turn diagonally and cut out armholes to fit. Sew fabric or paper roses to plastic hair band and round neck of tee shirt. Put arms through armholes and overlap interfacing at front, tucking base into white trousers. Wrap a length of ribbon round waist and tie in a bow.

Cupid

Starting at right side, pleat and tuck a length of lining fabric into a pair of swimming trunks, take excess over left shoulder, and tuck into back of trunks. Cut feather strips from folded tissue paper and glue to paper wings, trimming to fit. Glue wings to a length of gold braid and tie round head. Carry a toy bow and arrow, painted gold.

Wedding Cake

Cut hat pieces from paper. Fold 2cm down along side piece and snip, overlap ends by 2cm and glue to form a tube, then glue to top piece. Add elastic strap, then trim with ribbon, lace and figures. Make basic skirt from white fabric, and sew silver ribbon to hem. Wear with vest and add fabric swags, held in place with cake decorations.

Sweethearts

Using stamp from Valentine Balloons and fabric paints, print hearts all over vest or tee shirt, socks or tights. Cut pieces of card to fit inside, and leave paint to dry before turning over and printing other side. Print hair ribbon too. Wear with trousers, or net skirt, made from basic pattern, but using 3 times the waist measurement.

Food and Drink

Bouquet Sandwiches

BUTTER A SLICE OF WHITE BREAD AND CUT OFF CRUSTS.

ROLL INTO A CONE AND SECURE WITH A THIN RING CUT FROM A SMALL PEPPER.

FILL CONE WITH FINELY SHREDDED LETTUCE

PIPE ROSETTES OF TOMATO FLAVOURED CREAM CHEESE

Cupid Kisses

ROLL OUT READY-MADE PUFF PASTRY TO 3MM THICK AND CUT WITH 6CM WIDE HEART CUTTER

PUT 1 TEASPOON COTTAGE CHEESE AND WALNUT MIXTURE IN CENTRE OF HEART, MOISTEN EDGE AND TOP WITH ANOTHER HEART

BRUSH WITH BEATEN EGG AND LAY CROSS MADE FROM THIN STRIPS OF CHEESE OVER TOP

BAKE FOR 15 MINUTES AT 400°F/200°C/GAS MARK 6 AND SERVE HOT OR COLD

WOULD YOU LIKE A KISS, GEORGE?

Posy Mousse

MAKE UP A 570ML GREEN JELLY WITH 400ML BOILING WATER AND LEAVE UNTIL JUST BEGINNING TO SET

WHISK A CHILLED 170G TIN OF EVAPORATED MILK UNTIL THICK

FOLD JELLY INTO MILK, SPOON INTO 4 SMALL DISHES AND LEAVE TO SET

DECORATE WITH WHIPPED CREAM, SUGAR FLOWERS, AND STRAWBERRY FLAVOURED BOOTLACE BOW

YOU REALLY SHOULD WEAR SOMETHING MORE SENSIBLE IN THE KITCHEN, BROTHER DEAR!

Gingerbread Message Hearts

MAKE BASIC BISCUIT DOUGH, ADDING AN EXTRA 110G FLOUR, 2 HEAPED TEASPOONS GROUND GINGER AND MIXING 75G GOLDEN SYRUP INTO THE BEATEN EGG

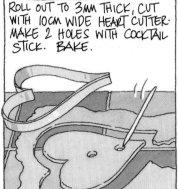

ROLL OUT TO 3MM THICK, CUT WITH 10CM WIDE HEART CUTTER. MAKE 2 HOLES WITH COCKTAIL STICK. BAKE.

WRITE MESSAGE ON PAPER, ROLL UP AND TIE TO HEART WITH RIBBON

HOW DO YOU SPELL 'PASSIONATELY', MUM?

Loving Cup

CUT STRAWBERRIES IN HALF, PUT IN ICE CUBE TRAY, FILL WITH PINK TINTED WATER AND FREEZE.

PEEL 6 WASHED LEMONS WITH POTATO PEELER THEN SQUEEZE LEMONS. MIX JUICE, PEEL, 225G SUGAR, AND 2 LITRES BOILING WATER IN BOWL AND LEAVE TO COOL.

STRAIN INTO JUG, COLOUR WITH PINK FOOD COLOURING AND CHILL IN FRIDGE

SERVE WITH HEART ICE CUBES AND LIPS STRAWS

Valentine Chocolate Box

MAKE, OR BUY, AN 18CM ROUND CAKE AND AN 18CM SQUARE CAKE. CUT TOPS LEVEL.

CUT THE ROUND CAKE IN HALF AND SLICE THROUGH ALL PIECES

ASSEMBLE WITH BUTTER ICING

FIX ONE HEART OFF CENTRE ON CAKE BOARD...

...AND OTHER ON STIFF CARD OF SAME SHAPE

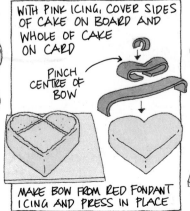

WITH PINK ICING, COVER SIDES OF CAKE ON BOARD AND WHOLE OF CAKE ON CARD

PINCH CENTRE OF BOW

MAKE BOW FROM RED FONDANT ICING AND PRESS IN PLACE

ICE ROSETTES OF BUTTER CREAM AND PRESS IN CHOCOLATES

FIX BOX TOP TO SIDE

Games

Catch a Bouquet

Make a small bouquet from artificial flowers. All the players stand in a circle, the bouquet is given to one of them, and another is chosen to stand in the middle. The bouquet is then thrown across the circle between players. When the person in the middle manages to catch it they change places with the player who threw it last.

With this Ring

Tie a brass curtain ring to a length of strong cotton and suspend from the top of a door frame. Blindfold one of the players, and point them towards the ring. The players shout directions — left, right, up, or down, to guide the blindfolded person's finger into the ring, who, when successful, is then allowed to name the next victim.

Love Me?

Make one less daisy than there are players. Everyone sits in a circle, and takes turns to tear a petal from the first daisy, saying 'loves me' or 'loves me not', before passing it to the player on their left. The one who tears off the last petal drops out. A new daisy is given to the next person, and play continues until the winner is left.

CHAPTER 3

Springtime Party

Decorations

Nest and Bunny Invitations, and Chick Napkin Ring

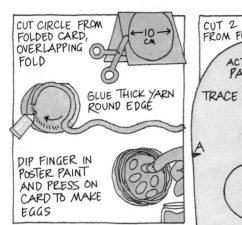

CUT CIRCLE FROM FOLDED CARD, OVERLAPPING FOLD

10 CM

GLUE THICK YARN ROUND EDGE

DIP FINGER IN POSTER PAINT AND PRESS ON CARD TO MAKE EGGS

CUT 2 BODIES AND 2 EARS FROM FELT

ACTUAL SIZE PATTERNS

TRACE ON TO CARD

BODY

A   B

EAR

OVERSEW BODIES TOGETHER FROM A TO B

6 CM

2 CM

12 CM

CUT SEMICIRCLE FROM FOLDED EDGE OF CARD AND GLUE BOTH FLAPS OF BUNNY INSIDE

GLUE ON EARS AND DRAW FACE

DECORATE CARD WITH PENS AND ADD DETAILS OF PARTY

It's Spring!

GLUE STRIP OF CARD INTO TUBE

4 CM

15 CM

DRAW FEET, AND GLUE ON COTTONWOOL BALL

DECORATE WITH STATIONARY STICKERS AND FOLDED DIAMOND OF CARD

PLACE ROUND NAPKIN

Cherry Blossom and Decorated Eggs

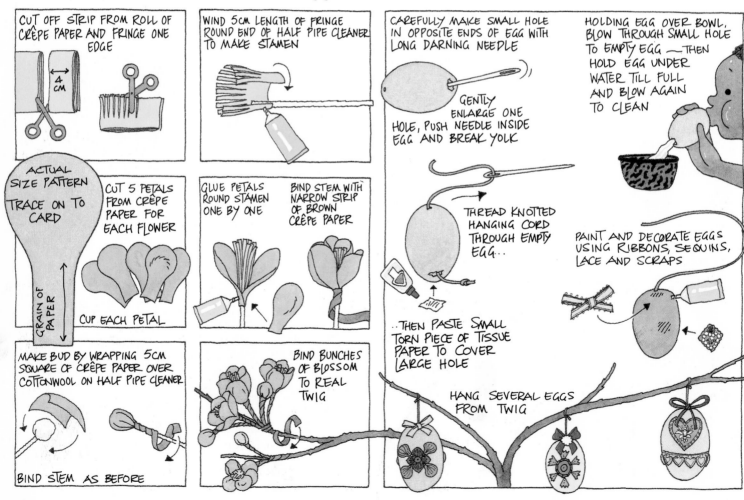

CUT OFF STRIP FROM ROLL OF CRÊPE PAPER AND FRINGE ONE EDGE

4 CM

WIND 5CM LENGTH OF FRINGE ROUND END OF HALF PIPE CLEANER TO MAKE STAMEN

CAREFULLY MAKE SMALL HOLE IN OPPOSITE ENDS OF EGG WITH LONG DARNING NEEDLE

GENTLY ENLARGE ONE HOLE, PUSH NEEDLE INSIDE EGG AND BREAK YOLK

HOLDING EGG OVER BOWL, BLOW THROUGH SMALL HOLE TO EMPTY EGG — THEN HOLD EGG UNDER WATER TILL FULL AND BLOW AGAIN TO CLEAN

ACTUAL SIZE PATTERN

TRACE ON TO CARD

GRAIN OF PAPER

CUT 5 PETALS FROM CRÊPE PAPER FOR EACH FLOWER

CUP EACH PETAL

GLUE PETALS ROUND STAMEN ONE BY ONE

BIND STEM WITH NARROW STRIP OF BROWN CRÊPE PAPER

THREAD KNOTTED HANGING CORD THROUGH EMPTY EGG...

...THEN PASTE SMALL TORN PIECE OF TISSUE PAPER TO COVER LARGE HOLE

PAINT AND DECORATE EGGS USING RIBBONS, SEQUINS, LACE AND SCRAPS

MAKE BUD BY WRAPPING 5CM SQUARE OF CRÊPE PAPER OVER COTTONWOOL ON HALF PIPE CLEANER

BIND STEM AS BEFORE

BIND BUNCHES OF BLOSSOM TO REAL TWIG

HANG SEVERAL EGGS FROM TWIG

Hatching Eggs Garland and Basket Plates

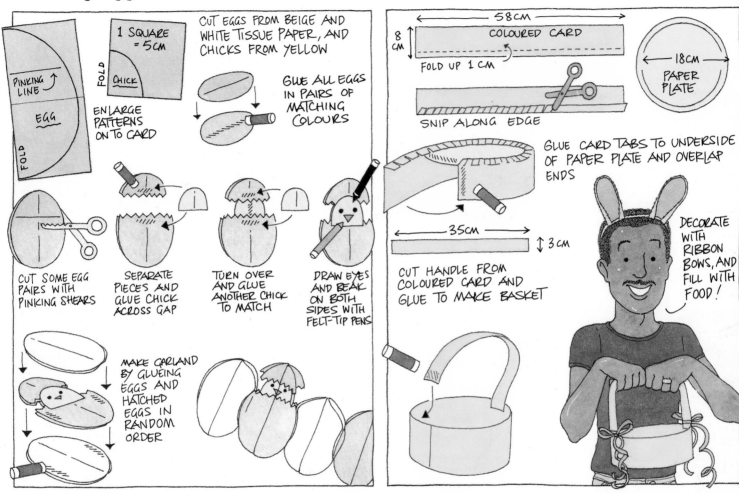

1 SQUARE = 5CM

PINKING LINE

EGG

FOLD

FOLD CHICK

ENLARGE PATTERNS ONTO CARD

CUT EGGS FROM BEIGE AND WHITE TISSUE PAPER, AND CHICKS FROM YELLOW

GLUE ALL EGGS IN PAIRS OF MATCHING COLOURS

CUT SOME EGG PAIRS WITH PINKING SHEARS

SEPARATE PIECES AND GLUE CHICK ACROSS GAP

TURN OVER AND GLUE ANOTHER CHICK TO MATCH

DRAW EYES AND BEAK ON BOTH SIDES WITH FELT-TIP PENS

MAKE GARLAND BY GLUEING EGGS AND HATCHED EGGS IN RANDOM ORDER

58CM

8 CM

COLOURED CARD

FOLD UP 1 CM

SNIP ALONG EDGE

18CM PAPER PLATE

GLUE CARD TABS TO UNDERSIDE OF PAPER PLATE AND OVERLAP ENDS

35CM

3CM

CUT HANDLE FROM COLOURED CARD AND GLUE TO MAKE BASKET

DECORATE WITH RIBBON BOWS, AND FILL WITH FOOD!

Daffodil Cups, Nest Plates, and Crocus Tablecloth

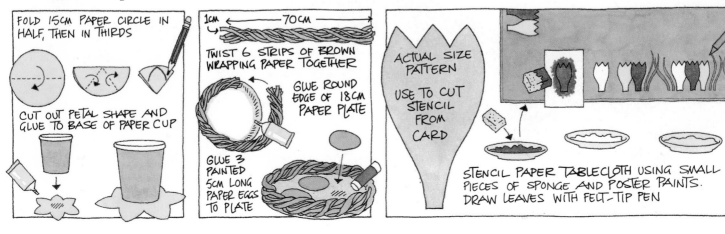

FOLD 15CM PAPER CIRCLE IN HALF, THEN IN THIRDS

CUT OUT PETAL SHAPE AND GLUE TO BASE OF PAPER CUP

1CM 70CM

TWIST 6 STRIPS OF BROWN WRAPPING PAPER TOGETHER

GLUE ROUND EDGE OF 18CM PAPER PLATE

GLUE 3 PAINTED 5CM LONG PAPER EGGS TO PLATE

ACTUAL SIZE PATTERN

USE TO CUT STENCIL FROM CARD

STENCIL PAPER TABLECLOTH USING SMALL PIECES OF SPONGE AND POSTER PAINTS. DRAW LEAVES WITH FELT-TIP PEN

23

Fancy Dress

Chick

BASIC SLEEVE PATTERN

1 CM CUT

FOLD OVER / FOLD OVER

FOLD

CUT 15CM SQUARE OF CARD FOR BEAK AND GLUE TO BASIC MASK

I *AM* SMILING, DADDY!

WEAR WITH TIGHTS

Lamb

FOLD

HAT
CUT 4 IN FLEECE

1 SQUARE = 10 CM

EAR
CUT 2 IN FELT

ENLARGE PATTERNS ON TO CARD AND CUT OUT TO MAKE HAT

30CM

TAIL
CUT 1 IN FLEECE

13 CM

WEAR WITH BLACK SWEATSHIRT AND LONG BLACK SOCKS

Make thigh length jacket in yellow fur fabric, using basic pattern, and elasticate hem to fit. Fasten opening with Velcro and sew base of jacket together in centre to form leg holes. Sew 3 scallops in each sleeve seam to make wings. Make basic mask in yellow, glue orange card beak to nose opening, and draw eyes with black pen.

Using basic patterns, make knee length trousers and jacket with elbow length sleeves in cream fleece fabric. Elasticate hems to fit, and fasten jacket opening with Velcro. Sew tail seam, gather ends and sew to back of jacket. Join shaped seams of hat, then stretch and sew 20cm of elastic to base of 2 sections. Sew ears in place.

Bunny

Using basic patterns, make jacket and trousers in fur fabric. Cut circle from fur fabric and gather edge. Stuff with wadding, draw up and sew to back of trousers for tail. Glue fur fabric to a plastic hair band. Cut 2 ears from fur fabric, and 2 from pink fabric. Sew together, leaving base open, turn to right side, and sew to band.

Hyacinth

Following pattern, cut flowers from crêpe paper and curl edge of petals. Glue ends together, then gather top edge round the end of a 10cm piece of thick green yarn. Bind top of flower with a narrow strip of green crêpe paper. Darn yarn on flowers into a green sweater and knitted hat until covered. Wear with green trousers and brown shoes.

Daffodil

Make top portion of basic mask, following measurements given here. Cut six petals from yellow card and glue to card strip, then gather orange crêpe paper to fit and glue in place. Glue pieces of green ribbon to ends and tie round head as a bonnet. Wear with a green leotard, and attach green ribbon leaves to ankles and wrists.

Chimney Pot Nest

Tear brown fabric into narrow strips and wind round base of knitted hat. Catch in place with a few stitches. Cut cups from a polystyrene egg box and sew to top of hat, together with two artificial birds. Cut the sleeves out of a red tee shirt and neaten edges. Draw brick lines with fabric paint and wear over a polo necked sweater.

Food and Drink

Chick and Bunny Rolls

CUT ROLLS IN HALF AND SPREAD WITH BUTTER

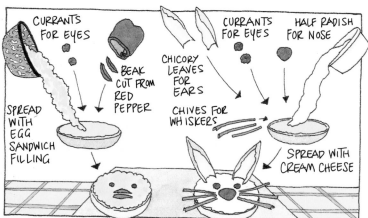
CURRANTS FOR EYES
SPREAD WITH EGG SANDWICH FILLING
BEAK CUT FROM RED PEPPER
CHICORY LEAVES FOR EARS
CHIVES FOR WHISKERS
CURRANTS FOR EYES
HALF RADISH FOR NOSE
SPREAD WITH CREAM CHEESE

DON'T EAT THEM, YET!

Bunny's Dip

CUT 4 AVOCADOS IN HALF, REMOVE STONES, SCOOP OUT FLESH AND MASH

MIX TOGETHER WITH—
3 TABLESPOONS PLAIN YOGURT
JUICE OF 2 LEMONS
SEASON TO TASTE
CLOVE OF CRUSHED GARLIC

STIR IN 2 CHOPPED HARD-BOILED EGGS, AND 2 CHOPPED TOMATOES

REMOVE THE CENTRE FROM A LARGE LETTUCE, FILL WITH BOWL OF DIP AND SERVE WITH RAW CARROT STICKS

Coconut Lambs

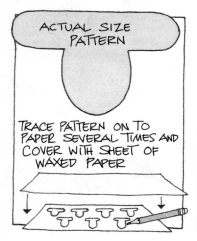
ACTUAL SIZE PATTERN
TRACE PATTERN ON TO PAPER SEVERAL TIMES AND COVER WITH SHEET OF WAXED PAPER

SPREAD MELTED COOKING CHOCOLATE INSIDE PATTERN LINES, LEAVE TO SET, THEN CAREFULLY PEEL OFF

CUT MINI SWISS ROLL IN HALF AND FIX TO ANOTHER WITH MELTED CHOCOLATE. PLACE ON WIRE TRAY
COVER WITH GLACÉ ICING THEN SPRINKLE WITH DESSICATED COCONUT

PRESS FACE AND CHOCOLATE STICK LEGS INTO ICING AND LEAVE TO SET

Chocolate Birds' Nests

GENTLY MELT 200g COOKING CHOCOLATE (TAKE CARE!) AND STIR IN 4 CRUSHED SHREDDED CEREAL BISCUITS

LIGHTLY OIL A 12 SECTION BUN TRAY

SPOON MIXTURE INTO TRAY, MAKING A DENT IN EACH NEST

PRESS 3 SUGAR EGGS IN EACH NEST, LEAVE TO SET, THEN REMOVE WITH A KNIFE

Spring Fever Punch

CUT STARS FROM LEMON RIND WITH A 3cm CUTTER AND MAKE A HOLE IN EACH

ROLL UP SMALL PIECES OF ORANGE RIND AND PUSH INTO HOLES

PLACE IN ICE CUBE TRAY, FILL WITH WATER AND FREEZE

MIX TOGETHER —
1½ LITRES ORANGE JUICE

½ LITRE GRAPEFRUIT JUICE

4 TABLESPOONS LIME CORDIAL

HALF FILL GLASS WITH CRUSHED ICE AND FILL UP WITH PUNCH. DECORATE WITH A DAFFODIL ICE CUBE

Nest of Chicks

FILL A SPONGE FLAN CASE WITH JAM AND WHIPPED CREAM, THEN TOP WITH ANOTHER

COVER WITH CHOCOLATE BUTTER CREAM AND PRESS BROKEN CHOCOLATE FLAKE INTO SIDES

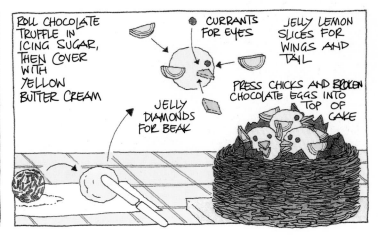

ROLL CHOCOLATE TRUFFLE IN ICING SUGAR, THEN COVER WITH YELLOW BUTTER CREAM

CURRANTS FOR EYES

JELLY LEMON SLICES FOR WINGS AND TAIL

PRESS CHICKS AND BROKEN CHOCOLATE EGGS INTO TOP OF CAKE

JELLY DIAMONDS FOR BEAK

Games

Hatch It!

The players divide into equal teams, stand in lines, and each leader is given a balloon. At the word "Go!" the balloon is passed over the head to the player behind, until it reaches the last in line, who has to sit on the balloon and burst it. This player then runs to the front and is the new leader. The team with most bursts wins.

Hopping Bunny

Players divide into pairs of bunnies, and one player in each pair is blindfolded. At the opposite end of the room is a line of carrots. The blindfolded players have to hop to the carrots, pick one up, and bring it back to their partner, who guides them by shouting directions. The ones with the most carrots after five minutes are the winners.

Fill the Nest

Paint four hard boiled eggs in different colours. Draw the nest target on a piece of card and place it on the floor. Mark four points, each 2 metres away from the nest, and divide the players into four teams. The first player in each team rolls their egg into the nest, and the score is taken. Play continues with the next in line.

CHAPTER 4

Fairies and Elves Party

Decorations

Leaf and Fairy Dust Invitations, and Ladybird Place Markers

CUT LEAF FROM PAPER AND MARK VEINS WITH EMPTY BALLPOINT PEN.

WRITE DETAILS IN THE SMALLEST WRITING POSSIBLE, AND GLUE ON SEQUIN DEWDROP

WRAP SOME GLITTER DUST IN A 15cm SQUARE OF CELLOPHANE. GATHER UP THE CORNERS, AND TIE TO LUGGAGE LABEL.

BEST QUALITY FAIRY DUST

WRITE PARTY DETAILS ON BACK OF LABEL.

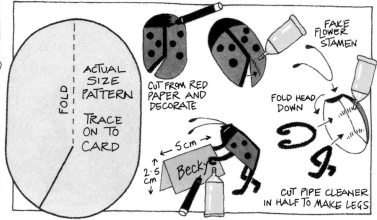

FOLD

ACTUAL SIZE PATTERN

TRACE ON TO CARD

CUT FROM RED PAPER AND DECORATE

FAKE FLOWER STAMEN

FOLD HEAD DOWN

Becky

5cm

2.5cm

CUT PIPE CLEANER IN HALF TO MAKE LEGS

Butterfly Garland and Firefly Lanterns

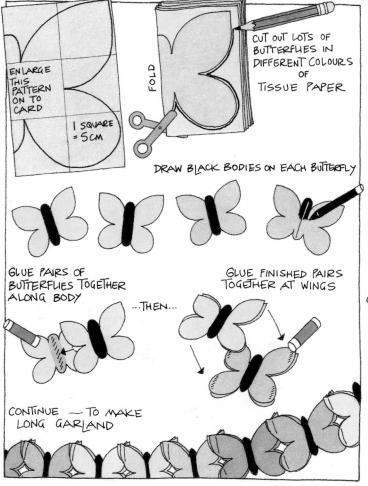

ENLARGE THIS PATTERN ON TO CARD

1 SQUARE = 5CM

FOLD

CUT OUT LOTS OF BUTTERFLIES IN DIFFERENT COLOURS OF TISSUE PAPER

DRAW BLACK BODIES ON EACH BUTTERFLY

GLUE PAIRS OF BUTTERFLIES TOGETHER ALONG BODY

...THEN...

GLUE FINISHED PAIRS TOGETHER AT WINGS

CONTINUE TO MAKE LONG GARLAND

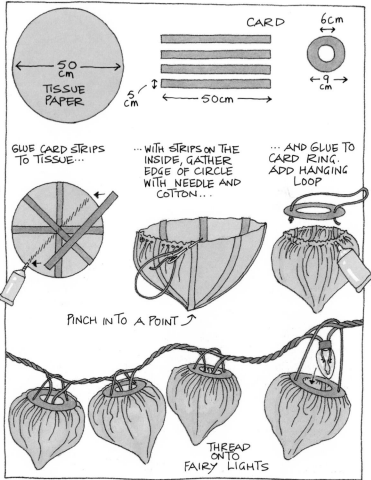

50 cm

TISSUE PAPER

CARD

6cm

9 cm

5 cm

50cm

GLUE CARD STRIPS TO TISSUE...

...WITH STRIPS ON THE INSIDE, GATHER EDGE OF CIRCLE WITH NEEDLE AND COTTON...

...AND GLUE TO CARD RING. ADD HANGING LOOP

PINCH IN TO A POINT ↑

THREAD ONTO FAIRY LIGHTS

Toadstool Stools and Bluebell Cups

CUT CIRCLE OF SPOTTY FABRIC 10CM BIGGER ALL ROUND THAN STOOL SEAT...

..TURN UNDER 5MM, THEN 1.5CM AND SEW DOWN, LEAVING SMALL OPENING.

THREAD WITH STRING

FOLD SHEET INTO SQUARE. PLACE STOOL IN CENTRE, AND BRING UP ALL EDGES UNTIL STOOL IS COVERED.

PLACE CIRCLE ONTO SEAT, PULLING STRING UNTIL TIGHT. TIE TO SECURE.

WRAP PAPER ROUND PAPER CUP

...AND...

TRACE THROUGH TO FIND BASE LINE

...THEN...

CUT ALONG BASE LINE

BRING ENDS OF LINE TOGETHER BY FOLDING, THEN FOLD AGAIN

...AND...

DRAW THIS SHAPE AND CUT OUT TO MAKE PATTERN

3CM

...THEN...

CUT OUT IN PAPER AND GLUE TO CUP

ACTUAL SIZE PATTERN TRACE ONTO CARD

FOLD

CUT OUT BUTTERFLY HANDLES FROM CARD AND DECORATE

...AND...

CURL OVER POINTS

FOLD WINGS AND GLUE IN PLACE

Spotty Cloth, Daisy Plates, Wand Markers, and Hat Napkins

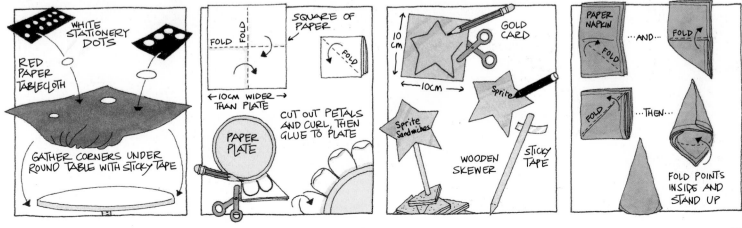

WHITE STATIONERY DOTS

RED PAPER TABLECLOTH

GATHER CORNERS UNDER ROUND TABLE WITH STICKY TAPE

FOLD

FOLD

SQUARE OF PAPER

FOLD

←10CM WIDER THAN PLATE→

PAPER PLATE

CUT OUT PETALS AND CURL, THEN GLUE TO PLATE

10 CM

←10CM→

GOLD CARD

Sprite

Sprite Sandwiches

WOODEN SKEWER

STICKY TAPE

PAPER NAPKIN

...AND...

FOLD

FOLD

FOLD

...THEN...

FOLD POINTS INSIDE AND STAND UP

Fancy Dress

Elf

COLLAR

BELLS

← 40CM →

HAT

40 CM

EAR PATTERN

1 SQUARE = 5CM

CUT 2 PAIRS EARS FROM FELT USING PATTERN

SEW, TURN TO RIGHT SIDE, PAD, AND JOIN OPENING —THEN QUILT.

BELL

ELASTIC →

WEAR WITH BELT, TEE SHIRT, RED TROUSERS AND BOOTS

Fairy

← 1½ TIMES CHEST →

BODICE

ADD TURNINGS ON ALL SIDES

UNDERARM TO HIP

SEQUIN STRAPS

WING PATTERN

FOLD

1 SQUARE = 10CM

30CM PIPE CLEANER

SEW TO BODICE

← 3 TIMES WAIST →

SKIRT

CUT 6 FROM NET

JOIN BACK SEAM ON EACH PIECE. PLACE ALL 6 TOGETHER AND MAKE SKIRT

ADD WAND, HEADBAND AND BALLET PUMPS

Make basic jacket, adding large buttons. Cut a circle of felt to fit across shoulders, and use jacket pattern to cut neck opening from centre. Trim as shown and sew to neck. Cut hat from felt, sew into cone to fit head, and trim away excess. Join ears in pairs, padding lightly, sew to sides of hat, and attach elastic to base of ears.

Cut rectangle of fabric as shown, hem top and bottom, machine stitch rows of shirring elastic, and join to form tube. Add sequin straps. Cut wings from 3 layers of net, machine stitch veins with silver thread, glue pipe cleaners to top edge and sew to back of bodice. Make basic skirt from 6 layers of net, and trim with sequins.

32

Ladybird

Cut a black fabric oval to fit back, plus turnings, and from red fabric an oval 10cm bigger all round. Decorate with black felt spots and stripe. Sew pieces together, gathering red piece to fit and leaving a space open. Turn to right side, stuff with wadding and close opening. Sew to back of tee shirt. Sew white felt spots on to beret.

Cobweb Sprite

Measure from left to right hand, arms outstretched, and cut a circle of black sheer fabric to fit. Cut a circle from centre to fit over head. With glitter paint, or fabric glue sprinkled with glitter dust, draw web pattern and push in sequins before set. Attach finger loops of elastic. Make headband from ribbon and 2 small half webs.

Butterfly

Cut wings from sheer fabric, colour with felt tipped pens and tack to tee shirt sleeves. Using swimming costume as a guide, cut 2 pieces from fur fabric, adding turnings. Sew side and crutch seams, and join shoulder straps with press studs or Velcro. Make antennae from millinery wire and wool bobbles and attach to plastic hair band.

Gnome

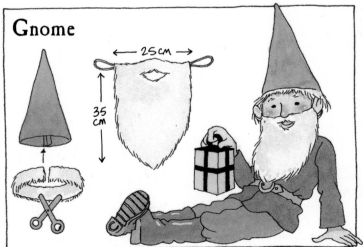

Make elf hat without ears, then sew a 5cm wide strip of white fur fabric under edge and trim to simulate hair. Cut beard and moustache from fur fabric and sew on elastic loops to fit round ears. Colour cheeks and nose with red lipstick, and whiten eyebrows with face paints. Wear with belted jacket, and trousers tucked into boots.

Food and Drink

Magical Mushrooms

MIX TOGETHER —

PINCH OF SALT

110G SELF RAISING FLOUR

110G SELF RAISING WHOLE MEAL FLOUR

RUB IN 40G BUTTER

ADD 50G WALNUT PIECES

THEN STIR IN 150ML MILK TO MAKE A SOFT DOUGH.

DIVIDE INTO 12 PIECES AND ROLL INTO BALLS. FLATTEN SLIGHTLY AND COOK ON BAKING TRAYS FOR 15 MINUTES AT 425°F/220°C/GAS MARK 7

SPLIT EACH SCONE IN HALF, SPREAD WITH CREAM CHEESE AND DECORATE WITH FORK.

PUSH HALF A COCKTAIL GHERKIN IN CENTRE OF EACH.

Cheese Wands and Sprite Sandwiches

CUT CHEESE INTO 1CM THICK SLICES AND CUT INTO STAR SHAPES WITH A 3CM CUTTER

MAKE A HOLE IN EACH STAR WITH A COCKTAIL STICK AND PUSH IN A SAVOURY STICK

USING A FAVOURITE FILLING, MAKE SANDWICHES AND REMOVE CRUSTS

CUT INTO SMALL TRIANGLES

USE WANDS TO MAKE SANDWICHES DISAPPEAR!

Meringue Toadstools

WHISK 2 EGG WHITES UNTIL THEY FORM STIFF PEAKS

GRADUALLY ADD 100G GRANULATED SUGAR, WHISKING UNTIL STIFF AND GLOSSY

LINE BAKING TRAYS WITH PARCHMENT AND PIPE 20 STEMS AND 20 CAPS. BAKE AT 275°F/140°C/GAS MARK 1 FOR 2 HOURS UNTIL DRY

STEMS   CAPS

COARSELY GRATE 1/3 OF 100G BAR WHITE CHOCOLATE, AND GENTLY HEAT REMAINDER

TRIM OFF TOPS OF STEMS, DIP INTO CHOCOLATE, FIX TO CAPS AND LEAVE TO SET.

GENTLY MELT 200G DARK CHOCOLATE AND DIP CAPS INTO COAT

SPRINKLE SOME WITH GRATED CHOCOLATE AND LEAVE TO SET

Butterfly Cakes

FOLLOW THE BASIC SMALL CAKE RECIPE. DIVIDE BETWEEN 16 CAKE CASES AND 16 PETIT FOUR CASES.

BAKE FOR 15 MINUTES AT 400°F/200°C/GAS MARK 6

CUT THE TOP OFF EACH CAKE, SPREAD WITH GLACÉ ICING AND DECORATE WITH JELLY SWEETS.

PIPE 2 ROSETTES OF BUTTER CREAM ON EACH CAKE. CUT TOPS IN HALF AND, WITH ROUND EDGES TOGETHER, PRESS IN PLACE.

Butterfly Cakes

Pixie Fancies

TRIM CHOCOLATE STICKS AND PRESS IN CENTRE OF WINGS.

Fairy Dew

POUR RED GRAPE JUICE INTO AN ICE CUBE TRAY AND FREEZE

POUR 150ML UNDILUTED BLACKCURRANT CORDIAL INTO LARGE JUG AND TOP UP WITH 2 LITRES CHERRYADE.

PLACE AN ICE CUBE INTO EACH CUP AND FILL WITH FAIRY DEW

WOULD ALL LADYBIRDS AND BUTTERFLIES PLEASE GO TO THE NEXT ROOM FOR THE GAMES!

YES, MRS. RIDING!

Elfin House

ADD 2 TABLESPOONS COCOA POWDER AND 75G CHOCOLATE DROPS TO BASIC PARTY CAKE MIXTURE

DIVIDE BETWEEN GREASED 1 LITRE BASIN AND 500ML JUG (BOTH OVENPROOF) AND BAKE FOR 50 MINUTES AT 325°F/170°C/GAS MARK 3

TRIM AND STICK JUG CAKE TO BOARD WITH CHOCOLATE SPREAD AND COVER WITH WHITE GLACÉ ICING

SPREAD CHOCOLATE ON BASIN CAKE, DECORATE WITH FORK AND PRESS IN PLACE

COVER TOP WITH RED GLACÉ ICING AND DECORATE WITH WHITE CHOCOLATE BUTTONS

MAKE FAIRIES FROM PINK JELLY BABIES WITH ALMOND FLAKE WINGS.

PRESS CHOCOLATE BISCUITS IN PLACE FOR DOOR AND WINDOW. ICE WINDOW FRAME AND ATTACH FAIRIES TO BOARD.

Games

Musical Wand

Make a wand from a garden cane and a foil paper star. The players sit in a circle and one person is given the wand. When the music starts the wand is passed clockwise from player to player, and when the music stops, whoever is holding the wand drops out. The winner is the last person left, who is given the wand and allowed to cast a spell!

Fairy Ring

Cut six cups from an egg box and glue each one to a wine cork. Paint red and decorate with white stationery dots. Glue the toadstools in the centre of a 50cm square of green card to form a circle. Mark a starting point in each corner from which tiddleywinks are shot into the fairy ring. The player with the most number of hits wins.

Flying Fairy

CUT FROM TISSUE PAPER

ACTUAL SIZE PATTERN

FOLD

Divide the players into two teams of goblins, and tie a length of ribbon between two chairs to separate them. Cut a fairy from tissue paper and drop her above the dividing line. For five minutes the teams have to keep the fairy flying, and out of their side, by blowing. Whenever she lands on the floor a point is counted against that side.

CHAPTER 5

Picnic Party

Decorations

Sandwich and Watermelon Invitations, and Hamper Napkin Ring

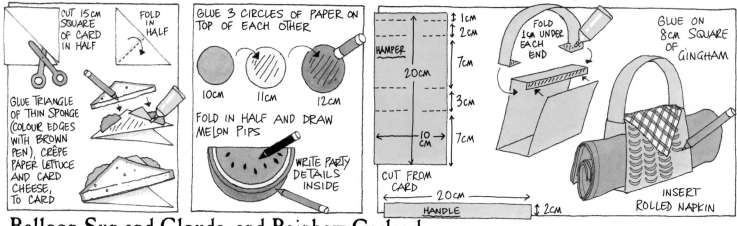

CUT 15 CM SQUARE OF CARD IN HALF

FOLD IN HALF

GLUE TRIANGLE OF THIN SPONGE (COLOUR EDGES WITH BROWN PEN), CRÊPE PAPER LETTUCE AND CARD CHEESE, TO CARD

GLUE 3 CIRCLES OF PAPER ON TOP OF EACH OTHER

10cm 11cm 12cm

FOLD IN HALF AND DRAW MELON PIPS

WRITE PARTY DETAILS INSIDE

1cm
2cm
HAMPER
20CM
7cm
3cm
10 CM
7cm
CUT FROM CARD
20CM
HANDLE
2cm

FOLD 1 CM UNDER EACH END

GLUE ON 8CM SQUARE OF GINGHAM

INSERT ROLLED NAPKIN

Balloon Sun and Clouds, and Rainbow Garland

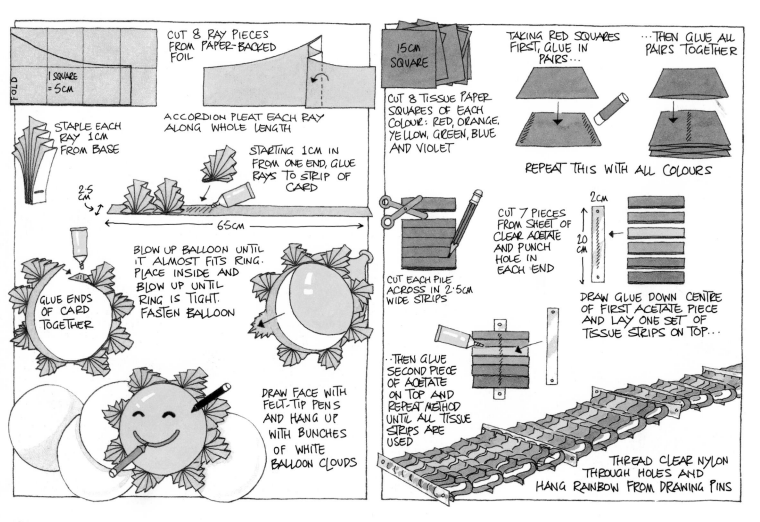

FOLD
1 SQUARE = 5CM

CUT 8 RAY PIECES FROM PAPER-BACKED FOIL

ACCORDION PLEAT EACH RAY ALONG WHOLE LENGTH

STAPLE EACH RAY 1 CM FROM BASE

STARTING 1CM IN FROM ONE END, GLUE RAYS TO STRIP OF CARD

2.5 CM

65CM

GLUE ENDS OF CARD TOGETHER

BLOW UP BALLOON UNTIL IT ALMOST FITS RING. PLACE INSIDE AND BLOW UP UNTIL RING IS TIGHT. FASTEN BALLOON

DRAW FACE WITH FELT-TIP PENS AND HANG UP WITH BUNCHES OF WHITE BALLOON CLOUDS

15CM SQUARE

CUT 8 TISSUE PAPER SQUARES OF EACH COLOUR: RED, ORANGE, YELLOW, GREEN, BLUE AND VIOLET

TAKING RED SQUARES FIRST, GLUE IN PAIRS...

...THEN GLUE ALL PAIRS TOGETHER

REPEAT THIS WITH ALL COLOURS

CUT EACH PILE ACROSS IN 2.5CM WIDE STRIPS

CUT 7 PIECES FROM SHEET OF CLEAR ACETATE AND PUNCH HOLE IN EACH END

2cm
20 CM

DRAW GLUE DOWN CENTRE OF FIRST ACETATE PIECE AND LAY ONE SET OF TISSUE STRIPS ON TOP...

...THEN GLUE SECOND PIECE OF ACETATE ON TOP AND REPEAT METHOD UNTIL ALL TISSUE STRIPS ARE USED

THREAD CLEAR NYLON THROUGH HOLES AND HANG RAINBOW FROM DRAWING PINS

Beehive Centrepiece and Sweetcorn Cups with Wheat Straws

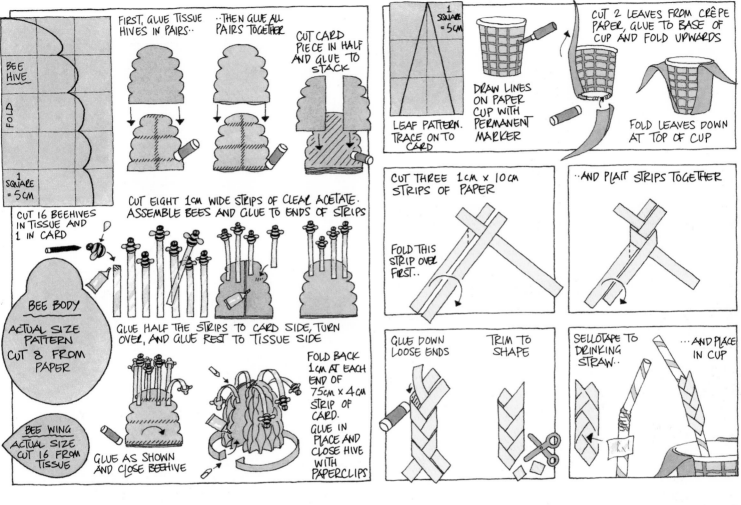

FIRST, GLUE TISSUE HIVES IN PAIRS...

...THEN GLUE ALL PAIRS TOGETHER

CUT CARD PIECE IN HALF AND GLUE TO STACK

BEE HIVE
FOLD
1 SQUARE = 5CM

CUT 16 BEEHIVES IN TISSUE AND 1 IN CARD

BEE BODY
ACTUAL SIZE PATTERN
CUT 8 FROM PAPER

BEE WING
ACTUAL SIZE
CUT 16 FROM TISSUE

CUT EIGHT 1CM WIDE STRIPS OF CLEAR ACETATE. ASSEMBLE BEES AND GLUE TO ENDS OF STRIPS

GLUE HALF THE STRIPS TO CARD SIDE, TURN OVER, AND GLUE REST TO TISSUE SIDE

GLUE AS SHOWN AND CLOSE BEEHIVE

FOLD BACK 1CM AT EACH END OF 75CM × 4CM STRIP OF CARD. GLUE IN PLACE AND CLOSE HIVE WITH PAPERCLIPS

1 SQUARE = 5CM

LEAF PATTERN. TRACE ON TO CARD

DRAW LINES ON PAPER CUP WITH PERMANENT MARKER

CUT 2 LEAVES FROM CRÊPE PAPER, GLUE TO BASE OF CUP AND FOLD UPWARDS

FOLD LEAVES DOWN AT TOP OF CUP

CUT THREE 1CM × 10CM STRIPS OF PAPER

FOLD THIS STRIP OVER FIRST...

...AND PLAIT STRIPS TOGETHER

GLUE DOWN LOOSE ENDS

TRIM TO SHAPE

SELLOTAPE TO DRINKING STRAW...

...AND PLACE IN CUP

Meadow Cloth, Field Poppies, and Cornflowers

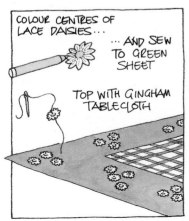

COLOUR CENTRES OF LACE DAISIES...

...AND SEW TO GREEN SHEET

TOP WITH GINGHAM TABLECLOTH

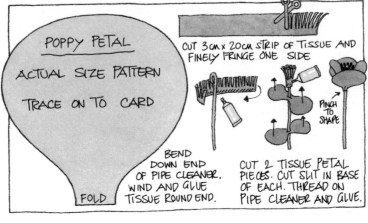

POPPY PETAL

ACTUAL SIZE PATTERN

TRACE ON TO CARD

FOLD

BEND DOWN END OF PIPE CLEANER. WIND AND GLUE TISSUE ROUND END.

CUT 3CM × 20CM STRIP OF TISSUE AND FINELY FRINGE ONE SIDE

PINCH TO SHAPE

CUT 2 TISSUE PETAL PIECES. CUT SLIT IN BASE OF EACH. THREAD ON PIPE CLEANER AND GLUE.

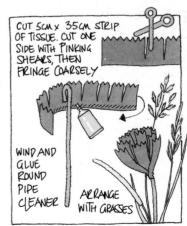

CUT 5CM × 35CM STRIP OF TISSUE. CUT ONE SIDE WITH PINKING SHEARS, THEN FRINGE COARSELY

WIND AND GLUE ROUND PIPE CLEANER

ARRANGE WITH GRASSES

39

Fancy Dress

Bumble Bee

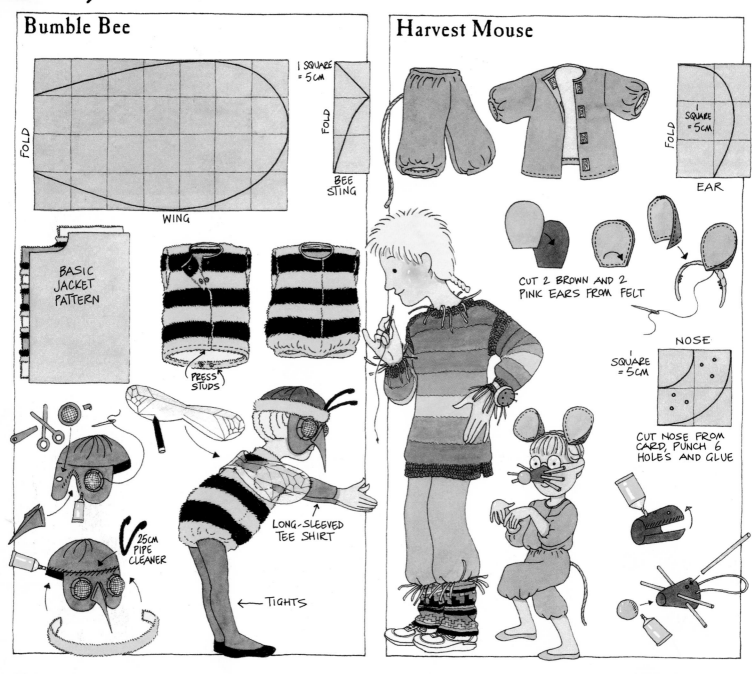

Harvest Mouse

Make sleeveless, thigh length basic jacket in striped fur fabric, made from joined strips. Elasticate hem and join together at centre to form leg holes. Remove handles from plastic tea strainers and sew to black basic mask. Glue on fur fabric strip, antennae, and sting. Cut wings from polythene, decorate with pen and sew to back and sleeves.

Make knee length trousers, inserting a pink cord tail in back seam, and a jacket with elbow length sleeves in brown velvet, using basic patterns. Elasticate hems to fit. Topstitch pairs of ears together, fold in half and sew to a plastic hair band. Glue pink table tennis ball to nose cone, thread holes with straws and fit elastic.

40

Thermos Flask

Placing centre front line on fold, and adding 5cm to back for opening, make sleeveless, full length basic jacket in checked fabric. Neaten neck edge with silver binding, and sew a length of 5cm wide white ribbon round jacket hem. Pleat and wind white silky scarf round neck. Make cup hat from a foil pudding basin and attach elastic chin strap.

Ant

Make a pair of shorts, and a short-sleeved, bolero length jacket in satin, using basic patterns. Elasticate hems to fit. Wear over long-sleeved tee shirt and tights. Stuff legs of another pair of tights and push through legs of shorts. Glue glossy paper circles to brown basic mask before cutting eye holes, then add nose and antennae.

Field Poppy

Make top portion of basic mask in green, with black card strip, inserting two lengths of 10cm wide fringed black crêpe paper behind card. Cut four petals from red taffeta lining, using the basic non-fray glue method, and sew a casing at base of each. Cut two pieces of elastic to fit round neck, thread each with two petals and secure ends.

Scarecrow

Sew a strip of wood across shoulders inside an oversize jacket, and wear with scruffy clothes, roughly patched with brightly coloured scraps of fabric. Cut a skein of straw-coloured raffia into 10m lengths and sew to narrow tape. Tack tape to inside of felt hat, under cuffs and hems, and round neck. Tack artificial birds to shoulders.

Food and Drink

Turf Squares

MIX TOGETHER—

250G CREAM CHEESE

4 TABLESPOONS FINELY CHOPPED FRESH MIXED HERBS

SEASON TO TASTE

BUTTER COLD SLICES OF WHOLEWHEAT TOAST, THEN THINLY SPREAD WITH YEAST EXTRACT

SPREAD THICKLY WITH HERB CHEESE AND SPRINKLE WITH CHOPPED PARSLEY

TRIM AWAY CRUSTS AND CUT INTO SQUARES

Caterpillars

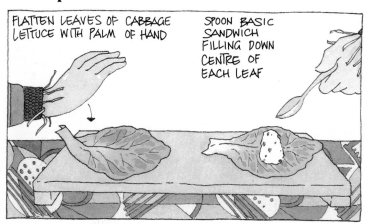

FLATTEN LEAVES OF CABBAGE LETTUCE WITH PALM OF HAND

SPOON BASIC SANDWICH FILLING DOWN CENTRE OF EACH LEAF

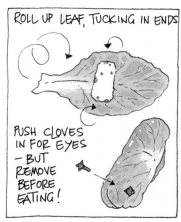

ROLL UP LEAF, TUCKING IN ENDS

PUSH CLOVES IN FOR EYES — BUT REMOVE BEFORE EATING!

ARRANGE ON BED OF RED LETTUCE LEAVES

Mud Pies

MELT 250G PLAIN CHOCOLATE AND USE HALF TO BRUSH THE INSIDE OF 12 CAKE CASES

REFRIGERATE UNTIL SET, THEN BRUSH WITH REMAINING CHOCOLATE. LEAVE TO SET, THEN CAREFULLY TEAR AWAY CASES

STIR 4 EGG YOLKS AND GRATED RIND OF 1 ORANGE INTO 150G MELTED CHOCOLATE

FOLD 4 WHISKED EGG WHITES INTO MIXTURE, FILL CASES, AND REFRIGERATE TO SET

Honeycomb Toffee

I KNOW YOU LIKE COOKING, YOUNG LADY, BUT THIS IS FOR ADULTS ONLY!

OH, MUM!

BOIL 50g DEMERARA SUGAR WITH 100g GOLDEN SYRUP IN LARGE SAUCEPAN FOR 5 MINUTES UNTIL RICH BROWN

QUICKLY STIR IN 2 LEVEL TEASPOONS BICARBONATE OF SODA — THE MIXTURE WILL DOUBLE IN SIZE! POUR INTO GREASED 15CM x 25CM TIN

WHEN ALMOST SET, GENTLY LOOSEN EDGES, CUT INTO SQUARES AND TURN ON TO RACK TO COOL

WHEN YOU'VE STOPPED SULKING, THERE'S TOFFEE TO TRY!

Dairy Milk Shake and Marzipan Bees

DISSOLVE 4 TABLESPOONS LIQUID HONEY IN 2 TABLESPOONS BOILING WATER

LIQUIDISE HONEY WITH 1½ LITRES MILK AND ½ LITRE VANILLA ICE CREAM

ROLL SMALL BALLS OF MARZIPAN FOR BEE HEADS AND BODIES AND PRESS TOGETHER

PAINT WITH FOOD COLOURING, AND PUSH IN ALMOND FLAKE WINGS. PRESS A BEE ON TO RIM OF EACH DRINK

HERE'S YOUR DRINK, SAM — WATCH OUT FOR THE BEE!

Picnic Basket

FIX 3 SLAB CAKES TOGETHER WITH VANILLA BUTTER CREAM, THEN SPREAD REMAINDER OVER SIDES. MARK PATTERN WITH FORK

PLAIT STRIPS OF BASIC BISCUIT DOUGH. CUT TO FIT SIDES OF BASKET AND FORM A HANDLE. BAKE AND LEAVE TO COOL

COVER MINI SWISS ROLL WITH GLACÉ ICING, TRIM BASE AND FIX TO TOP OF CAKE

COVER EGG BOX CUP WITH FOIL AND FIT ON TOP OF FLASK. PRESS PLAITS IN PLACE

ROLL 250g FONDANT ICING TO 5MM THICK, CUT 23CM SQUARE AND PRESS ON TOP OF CAKE

PAINT GINGHAM CHECKS WITH FOOD COLOURING

Games

Rainbow Artists

Draw a rainbow outline on a sheet of paper for each team and pin to a wall. Line the teams up at the opposite end of the room and give the first players a box of seven coloured pens. At the word 'Go' they run up to their rainbow, colour in one section completely, run back, and hand the pens to the next player. The quickest team wins.

In My Basket

One player thinks of an item to take on a picnic — for example, a rug — and says, 'I went on a picnic and packed a rug in my basket.' The next player repeats the sentence, adding another item after 'rug'. This way the list gets longer, and more difficult to remember. When one player forgets an item, they drop out and a new list is started.

Worm Pictures

This is a game for two players who are given a sheet of paper and a different coloured pencil each. They both draw five wriggly worms, and then exchange papers with their opposite player. A limit of three minutes is set, during which time the players have to draw a picture, incorporating all the worms in the most inventive way.

CHAPTER 6

Seaside Party

Decorations

Starfish and Sandcastle Invitations, and Shrimp Serviettes

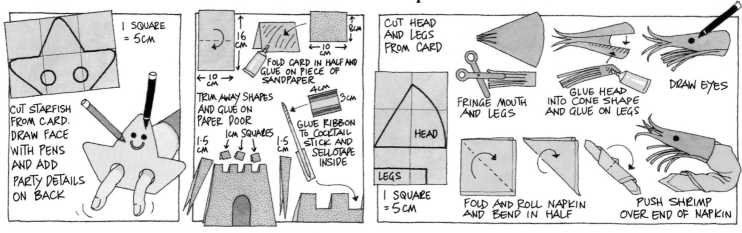

1 SQUARE = 5CM

CUT STARFISH FROM CARD. DRAW FACE WITH PENS AND ADD PARTY DETAILS ON BACK

16 CM

10 CM

10 CM

8CM

10 CM

FOLD CARD IN HALF AND GLUE ON PIECE OF SANDPAPER

TRIM AWAY SHAPES AND GLUE ON PAPER DOOR

1.5 CM

1CM SQUARES

1.5 CM

4CM

3CM

GLUE RIBBON TO COCKTAIL STICK AND SELLOTAPE INSIDE

CUT HEAD AND LEGS FROM CARD

HEAD

LEGS

1 SQUARE = 5CM

FRINGE MOUTH AND LEGS

GLUE HEAD INTO CONE SHAPE AND GLUE ON LEGS

DRAW EYES

FOLD AND ROLL NAPKIN AND BEND IN HALF

PUSH SHRIMP OVER END OF NAPKIN

Deckchair Placemarkers and Seashell Lights

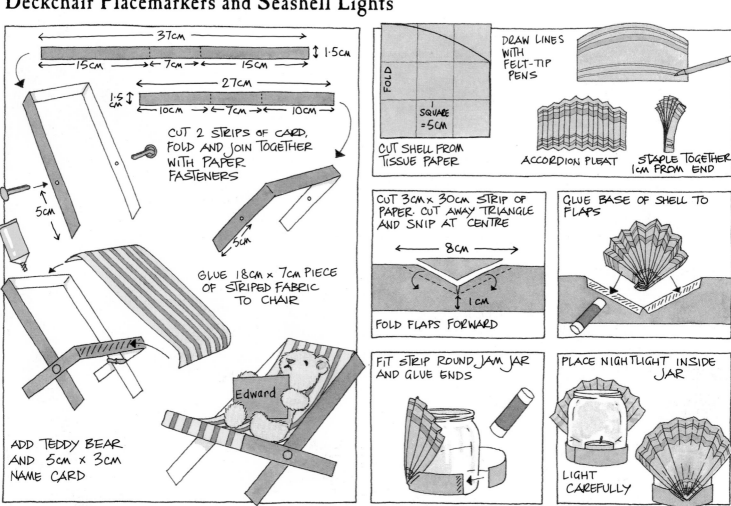

37CM

1.5CM

15CM — 7CM — 15CM

27CM

1.5 CM

10CM — 7CM — 10CM

CUT 2 STRIPS OF CARD, FOLD AND JOIN TOGETHER WITH PAPER FASTENERS

5CM

5CM

5CM

GLUE 18CM × 7CM PIECE OF STRIPED FABRIC TO CHAIR

Edward

ADD TEDDY BEAR AND 5CM × 3CM NAME CARD

FOLD

1 SQUARE = 5CM

CUT SHELL FROM TISSUE PAPER

DRAW LINES WITH FELT-TIP PENS

ACCORDION PLEAT

STAPLE TOGETHER 1CM FROM END

CUT 3CM × 30CM STRIP OF PAPER. CUT AWAY TRIANGLE AND SNIP AT CENTRE

8CM

1CM

FOLD FLAPS FORWARD

GLUE BASE OF SHELL TO FLAPS

FIT STRIP ROUND JAM JAR AND GLUE ENDS

PLACE NIGHTLIGHT INSIDE JAR

LIGHT CAREFULLY

Shoal of Fish Garland and Crab Platters

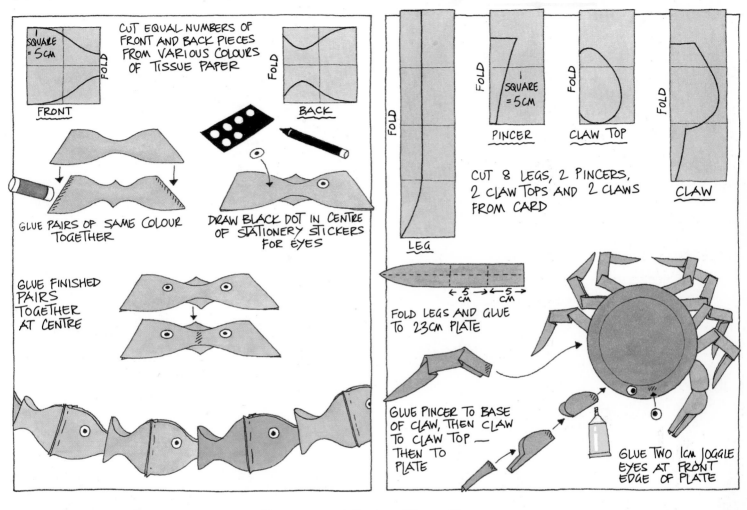

1 SQUARE = 5CM
FOLD
FRONT

CUT EQUAL NUMBERS OF FRONT AND BACK PIECES FROM VARIOUS COLOURS OF TISSUE PAPER

FOLD
BACK

GLUE PAIRS OF SAME COLOUR TOGETHER

DRAW BLACK DOT IN CENTRE OF STATIONERY STICKERS FOR EYES

GLUE FINISHED PAIRS TOGETHER AT CENTRE

FOLD
LEG

FOLD
1 SQUARE = 5CM
PINCER

FOLD
CLAW TOP

FOLD
CLAW

CUT 8 LEGS, 2 PINCERS, 2 CLAW TOPS AND 2 CLAWS FROM CARD

FOLD LEGS AND GLUE TO 23CM PLATE
5 CM   5 CM

GLUE PINCER TO BASE OF CLAW, THEN CLAW TO CLAW TOP — THEN TO PLATE

GLUE TWO 1CM JOGGLE EYES AT FRONT EDGE OF PLATE

Fishing Net Cloth, Bucket Cups, and Palm Tree Straws

SEW CORKS TO EDGE OF GARDEN MESH AND PLACE OVER CLOTH

GLUE PAPER FISH TO BLUE PAPER TABLECLOTH

PUSH PAPER FASTENERS THROUGH ENDS OF 1.5CM x 18CM PAPER STRIP

FOLD ENDS DOWN

GLUE TO PAPER CUP

FOLD
12CM PAPER SQUARE

FOLD

FOLD

1.5 CM

CUT OFF POINT

FRINGE CUT EDGE

OPEN OUT, PUSH ON TO STRAW AND GLUE IN PLACE

Fancy Dress

Mermaid

King Neptune

Sew and quilt shell pieces, then sew to bikini top, taking a dart from base if needed. Cut out tail pieces, following diagram, and join as for shells. Stuff lightly, quilt tail, draw scale pattern, and dart top edge to fit waist. Join at back with Velcro. Wear over basic long skirt made from crumpled fabric decorated with seashells.

Hem all cut edges of robe, then gather shoulders and trim. Wear over swimming trunks, and tie waist with dressing gown cord. Cut seaweed from green polythene rubbish bag and glue under base of crown. Sew seaweed to length of narrow tape, and glue ends to crown to make beard. Cut trident from card and glue to bamboo cane.

Octopus

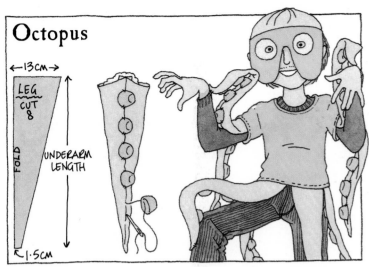

Fold each leg piece in half and join long seam. Turn to right side, stuff lightly and join opening. Sew egg box cup suckers along legs. Sew to tee shirt – 2 to each sleeve, and 4 to base. Wear over black trousers and sweater, catching legs with a few stiches. Make basic mask in pale green and paint eyes with poster paints.

Ice Cream Sundae

Lengthen white tee shirt by sewing on strips of satin, then elasticate base. Cut chocolate sauce collar from satin circle, using the basic non-fray glue method. Join wafer pieces, stuff and quilt, then sew to a hair band. Elasticate 47cm circle of white lawn to fit head, then cut a slit for wafer and neaten. Sew bobble cherry on top.

Bathing Belle

Make basic jacket with short sleeves and knee length basic trousers from printed cotton. Also cut a 55cm diameter circle for mob cap. Turn up hems and sew on top of wide ric rac braid. Work 3 rows of shirring elastic round waist, then work 2 rows of shirring 5cm up from sleeve and trouser hems, and 5cm in from edge of cap.

Pirate

Make eyepatch from black paper and elastic. Tie spotted handkerchief round head and hang brass curtain rings over ears with loops of thread. Sew felt squares to tongues of canvas shoes and trim with gold buckles. Wear with stripy tee shirt and socks, and trousers cut just below knee. Tie a silky scarf round waist and tuck in a toy sword.

Food and Drink

Oyster and Whelk Sandwiches

TOAST BREAD SLICES ON ONE SIDE. TURN OVER, BUTTER AND TRIM AWAY CRUSTS. CUT WITH FLUTED CUTTER.

SPREAD ONE PIECE THICKLY WITH CREAM CHEESE, ADD A COCKTAIL ONION AND TOP WITH ANOTHER PIECE

SLICE LOAF LENGTHWISE. BUTTER SLICES AND SPREAD WITH FILLING. REMOVE CRUSTS.

CUT IN HALF DIAGONALLY AND ROLL UP

Croissant Crabs

SLICE MINI CROISSANT OPEN. BUTTER AND SPREAD WITH FILLING.

CUT 2 FRONT CLAWS FROM CHEESE SLICES, AND 8 LEGS FROM PEPPER STRIPS, AND INSERT

MAKE HOLES WITH COCKTAIL STICK AND PRESS IN CURRANT EYES

KING NEPTUNE'S MOTHER WOULD LIKE HIM TO RETURN ALL CRABS TO THE KITCHEN!

Treasure Chests

ADD 2 TABLESPOONS COCOA POWDER TO BASIC SMALL CAKE MIXTURE AND BAKE IN 15CM X 30CM TIN

CUT CHOCOLATE COVERED MINI SWISS ROLLS IN HALF, THEN CUT CAKE IN STRIPS TO MATCH

DIP SIDES OF CAKE IN MELTED CHOCOLATE AND LEAVE ON RACK TO SET

ICE BUTTER CREAM ON TOP OF CAKE, PRESS IN CHOCOLATE COINS AND JELLY SWEETS, AND TOP WITH SWISS ROLL.

Rockpool Trifles

BREAK SPONGE CAKE INTO ROCK SHAPES AND PLACE IN BOTTOM OF GLASS DISHES

MAKE GREEN JELLY AND ADD A FEW DROPS OF BLUE COLOURING, THEN POUR OVER SPONGE TO SOAK.

PRESS IN SHRIMP SWEETS, MARZIPAN STARFISH AND ANGELICA SEAWEED AND LEAVE TO SET IN FRIDGE

TOP UP WITH REMAINING JELLY AND LEAVE TO SET

Deep Blue Sea

DIP RIMS OF GLASSES IN EGG WHITE, THEN IN DEMERARA SUGAR AND LEAVE TO DRY

MIX A FEW DROPS OF BLUE COLOURING INTO 2 LITRES OF FIZZY LEMONADE AND POUR INTO GLASSES

TOP WITH A SCOOP OF VANILLA ICE CREAM AND ADD A PALM TREE STRAW

CREW REPORTING FOR DRINKS, CAP'N LUCY!

Sponge Sandcastle

MAKE DOUBLE QUANTITY OF BASIC PARTY CAKE MIXTURE AND BAKE IN TWO 15CM x 30CM TINS. CUT CAKES IN HALF AND SANDWICH TOGETHER WITH JAM

FIX A SWISS ROLL TO EACH CORNER WITH BUTTER CREAM, THEN SPREAD REMAINDER OVER WHOLE CAKE

PRESS TOASTED CHOPPED NUTS INTO ICING

DECORATE WITH CHOCOLATE BISCUITS, SHELL CHOCOLATES AND SWEET PEBBLES

PUSH A FLAG IN EACH TURRET

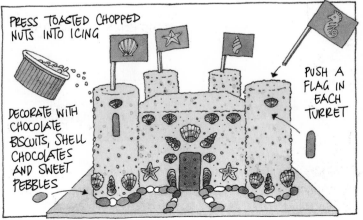

Games

Fish For Gold

Cut out 20 boots, 20 fish, and a treasure chest from paper. Attach a metal paper clip to each shape, and place in a plastic bucket. Give each player a magnet rod and arrange them round the bucket. Everyone fishes until the bucket is empty and scores 5 points for each boot, 10 points for each fish, and 25 points for the treasure.

Man Overboard!

The players sit in a circle round an inflated lifebelt, and one is given a small rag doll. When the music starts the doll is passed clockwise until the music stops. The person holding the doll then has to throw it into the lifebelt to stay in the game. If the doll falls outside, they drop out, and play continues with the next player.

Message Bottles

Arrange ten clear plastic bottles as shown and put a piece of paper in each one showing how much you score if you knock it over. Mark a point 3 metres away from the front bottle with a piece of tape, and the players take it in turns to roll a small ball at the bottles. Someone keeps the score, and the first to reach 500 is the winner.

CHAPTER 7

Funfair Party

Decorations

Tent and Crystal Ball Invitations, and Fairground Bunting

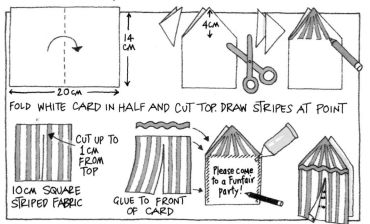

FOLD WHITE CARD IN HALF AND CUT TOP. DRAW STRIPES AT POINT

14 CM

4 CM

20 CM

CUT UP TO 1 CM FROM TOP

10 CM SQUARE STRIPED FABRIC

GLUE TO FRONT OF CARD

Please come to a Funfair party!

CUT SILVER FOIL CARD CIRCLE AND TWO 2CM x 5CM PIECES OF BLACK CARD

GLUE TO FRONT

10 CM

TRIM, FOLD AND GLUE TO BACK

Look into the future... Please come to a

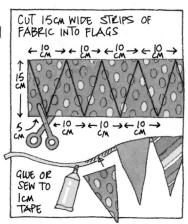

CUT 15CM WIDE STRIPS OF FABRIC INTO FLAGS

10 CM   10 CM   10 CM   10 CM

15 CM

5 CM   10 CM   10 CM   10 CM

GLUE OR SEW TO 1CM TAPE

Clown Garland and Windmill Place Markers

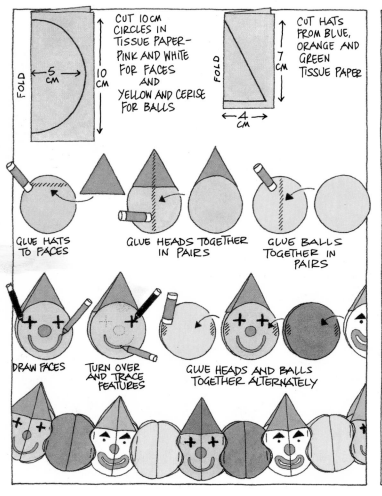

CUT 10CM CIRCLES IN TISSUE PAPER - PINK AND WHITE FOR FACES AND YELLOW AND CERISE FOR BALLS

FOLD   5 CM   10 CM

CUT HATS FROM BLUE, ORANGE AND GREEN TISSUE PAPER

FOLD   7 CM   4 CM

GLUE HATS TO FACES

GLUE HEADS TOGETHER IN PAIRS

GLUE BALLS TOGETHER IN PAIRS

DRAW FACES

TURN OVER AND TRACE FEATURES

GLUE HEADS AND BALLS TOGETHER ALTERNATELY

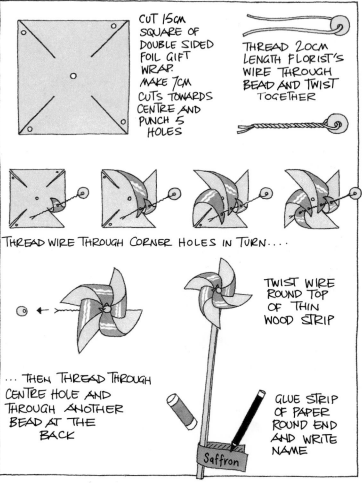

CUT 15CM SQUARE OF DOUBLE SIDED FOIL GIFT WRAP. MAKE 7CM CUTS TOWARDS CENTRE AND PUNCH 5 HOLES

THREAD 20CM LENGTH FLORIST'S WIRE THROUGH BEAD AND TWIST TOGETHER

THREAD WIRE THROUGH CORNER HOLES IN TURN....

TWIST WIRE ROUND TOP OF THIN WOOD STRIP

... THEN THREAD THROUGH CENTRE HOLE AND THROUGH ANOTHER BEAD AT THE BACK

GLUE STRIP OF PAPER ROUND END AND WRITE NAME

Saffron

54

Big Top Streamers and Daredevil Dolls

CUT EIGHT 9CM WIDE STRIPS IN RED, AND EIGHT IN YELLOW CRÊPE PAPER

CUT SCALLOP BORDER FROM FOLDED CREPE PAPER

5 CM

12 CM

12CM

GLUE RED STRIPS TO BACK OF 23CM PAPER PLATE

GLUE YELLOW STRIPS BETWEEN RED STRIPS

STICKY TAPE CORD TO CENTRE OF PLATE AND HANG UP

TIE STRING TO LENGTHS OF DOWEL FOR TRAPEZE AND SEW FEET OR HANDS OF TOYS SECURELY IN PLACE

SUSPEND BY LENGTH OF COTTON

SEW COCKTAIL PARASOL TO HAND

PIN ENDS OF STRING TAUT THEN SEW FEET TO TIGHTROPE

TAPE POLYSTYRENE TILE TO CARDBOARD AND COVER WITH FABRIC. TRAP ARMS AND LEGS OF TOY WITH RIBBON AND DRAWING PINS

PUSH COCKTAIL DAGGERS AROUND TOY

Food Stalls, Balloon Plates, Bow Napkins, and Stilt Straws

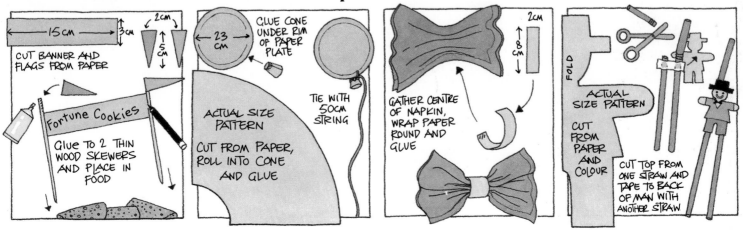

15 CM

3 CM

2 CM

5 CM

CUT BANNER AND FLAGS FROM PAPER

Fortune Cookies

Glue TO 2 THIN WOOD SKEWERS AND PLACE IN FOOD

23 CM

GLUE CONE UNDER RIM OF PAPER PLATE

2CM

ACTUAL SIZE PATTERN

CUT FROM PAPER, ROLL INTO CONE AND GLUE

TIE WITH 50CM STRING

8 CM

2cm

GATHER CENTRE OF NAPKIN, WRAP PAPER ROUND AND GLUE

FOLD

ACTUAL SIZE PATTERN

CUT FROM PAPER AND COLOUR

CUT TOP FROM ONE STRAW AND TAPE TO BACK OF MAN WITH ANOTHER STRAW

Fancy Dress

Clowns

Cut collar and cuffs from an old shirt and wear over a vest or tee shirt, adding bow tie and card shirt front. Make baggy basic trousers, thread waist casing with hoop of dressmaker's boning, and hold up with braces. Make basic mask and add painted egg box cup nose and fringed paper hair. Make hat by adding paper ring to fit head.

White Face

Make basic trousers and jacket, without tapering sleeves and trouser legs, and work 2 rows of shirring 10cm up from hems. Fold net in half and sew 1.5cm in from fold. Thread casing with 1cm elastic to fit neck and join ends. Sew hat seam, adjusting to fit head, gather top and add elastic strap. Sew wool bobbles to hat and jacket front.

Big Top

Cut striped fabric to fit one and a half times round hips, and from shoulders to floor, adding turnings. Hem sides and base, and make a casing at top. Cut armholes and neaten raw edges. Thread cord through casing. Glue hat into cone, draw on stripes, and glue jumbo ric rac braid under rim. Add elastic strap and paper pennant.

Strong Man

Wear swimming trunks over tights and long-sleeved vest, tacking fancy braid round neck and cuffs. Push a rolled up pair of socks down each sleeve to make muscles. Draw moustache with eyebrow pencil and slick hair down with gel. Tape a black balloon to each end of a garden cane, then wind cane with strip of black crêpe paper to cover.

Escapologist

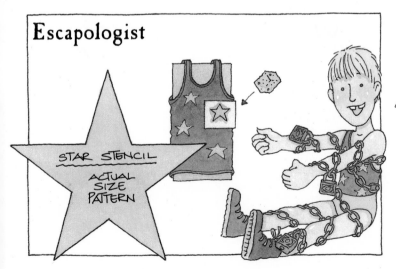

Slip singlet over a rectangle of card. Cut stencil from a piece of card and decorate singlet with stars, dabbing on fabric paint with a sponge, and allowing one side to dry before turning over and decorating reverse. Wear with swimming trunks and ankle boots. Wrap body, arms, and legs with plastic garden chain, and fasten with padlocks.

Fortune Teller

Fold headscarf diagonally, sew gold coin sequins to fold, and tie round head. Make shawl from a square of fabric edged with lampshade fringing. Make basic long skirt and wear with patterned apron. Paint a 15cm ball silver and glue to a black painted cream cheese carton. Wear gold hoop earrings and tuck a pack of cards in apron pocket.

Food and Drink

Lucky Popcorn Dip

MIX 1 TABLESPOON OIL AND 200G POPPING CORN IN HEAVY SAUCEPAN, COVER WITH LID AND PLACE ON HIGH HEAT.

SHAKE PAN AS CORN STARTS TO POP. REMOVE FROM HEAT WHEN POPPING SOUNDS STOP

EMPTY INTO BOWL AND STIR IN 75G MELTED BUTTER AND SALT TO TASTE

CUT SHAPES FROM CHEESE SLICES, MIX WITH POPCORN AND PILE INTO PAPER CUPS

Clown Rolls

CUT AND BUTTER ROUND AND OVAL ROLLS, AND SPREAD WITH CREAM CHEESE FILLING

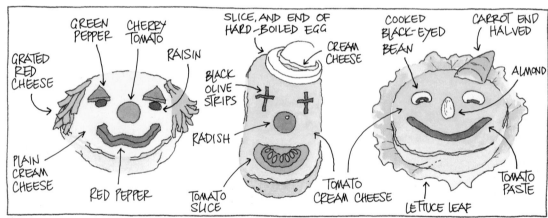

GREEN PEPPER — CHERRY TOMATO — RAISIN — GRATED RED CHEESE — SLICE, AND END OF HARD-BOILED EGG — CREAM CHEESE — BLACK OLIVE STRIPS — COOKED BLACK-EYED BEAN — CARROT END HALVED — ALMOND — PLAIN CREAM CHEESE — RED PEPPER — RADISH — TOMATO SLICE — TOMATO CREAM CHEESE — LETTUCE LEAF — TOMATO PASTE

Fortune Cookies

GENTLY MELT 80G GOLDEN SYRUP, 60G BUTTER AND 60G CASTER SUGAR IN A SAUCEPAN

REMOVE FROM HEAT AND STIR IN 60G PLAIN FLOUR AND ½ TEASPOON GROUND GINGER

PLACE TEASPOONS OF MIXTURE ON LINED BAKING SHEET AND BAKE FOR 10 MINUTES AT 325°F/170°C/ GAS MARK 3

LEAVE TO COOL FOR A FEW SECONDS, FOLD OVER 5CM x 1CM PAPER MESSAGES AND LEAVE TO SET

you will meet a handsome clown

Dodgem Doughnuts

CUT WEDGE FROM MINI DOUGHNUT, THEN COVER WITH GLACÉ ICING 	ADD HEADLIGHTS, RADIATOR AND STEERING WHEEL CUT FROM LIQUORICE ALLSORTS 	PUSH TUBE WAFER INTO BACK OF CAR 	PENNY! LEAVE SOME FOR THE GUESTS! 

Fairground Frappé

FREEZE 1 LITRE PINEAPPLE JUICE IN ICE CUBE TRAYS 	MIX 4 TABLESPOONS TINNED CREAM OF COCONUT WITH 4 TABLESPOONS HOT WATER AND LEAVE TO COOL 	PLACE PINEAPPLE ICE CUBES IN PLASTIC BAG, CRUSH WITH ROLLING PIN, AND HALF FILL GLASSES WITH ICE 	STIR COCONUT MIXTURE INTO 1 LITRE CREAM SODA AND TOP UP GLASSES 

Carousel Cake

CUT 23CM FOIL PLATE AND BEND TO MAKE CONE WITH 20CM BASE 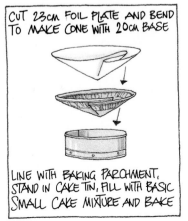 LINE WITH BAKING PARCHMENT, STAND IN CAKE TIN, FILL WITH BASIC SMALL CAKE MIXTURE AND BAKE	COVER TOP OF 20CM SPONGE, AND 12CM PIECE OF SWISS ROLL, WITH FONDANT ICING  FIT TOGETHER WITH 3 WOODEN SKEWERS	COVER CONE CAKE WITH FONDANT ICING, PLACE ON CAKE BOARD AND FIX TO SWISS ROLL WITH BUTTER CREAM 	FIX FIVE 12CM CANDY CANES ROUND CAKE WITH BUTTER CREAM AND ADD TOY ANIMALS  TRIM WITH STRIPS OF GIFT WRAP

59

Games

Clown Hoop-La

Cut face from corrugated card, paint with white emulsion paint and leave to dry. Stick on plastic self adhesive hooks, then paint features, hair and hat with poster paints. Pin on wall and mark a line 2 metres away. Each player throws seven 6cm diameter fibre plumber's washers at the board, scoring 5 points for each ring on a hook.

Bouncy Goldfish

Using poster paints, paint a goldfish on each of five table tennis balls and leave to dry. Line up ten empty jam jars on a hard floor, and mark a point 3 metres away. The players form 2 teams and take it in turns to bounce the goldfish balls on the floor towards the jars. Every time a goldfish jumps into a jar, 10 points are scored.

Star Ring

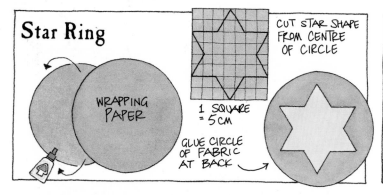

Cut a 50cm diameter circle of corrugated card and cover with wrapping paper. Cut star from centre, glue piece of fabric behind star, then cut slits in centre with craft knife. Hang ring from doorway with 2 pieces of string. The players stand 2 metres away and take turns to throw a ball through the star, winning a small gift for each hit.

CHAPTER 8

Outer Space Party

Decorations

Constellation and Telescope Invitations, and Space Belts

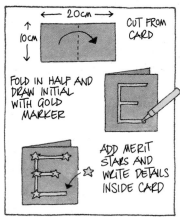

20cm

10cm

CUT FROM CARD

FOLD IN HALF AND DRAW INITIAL WITH GOLD MARKER

ADD MERIT STARS AND WRITE DETAILS INSIDE CARD

15cm

10cm

CUT 2 IN CARD AND 2 IN STARRY WRAPPING PAPER

FOLD PAPER PIECES IN HALF AND GLUE TO STARRY CARD

GLUE PAPER TO ONE PIECE OF CARD, AND 8cm PAPER CIRCLE TO CENTRE OF THAT. WRITE PARTY DETAILS ON CIRCLE

CUT 4cm HOLE FROM REMAINING CARD, EDGE WITH SILVER MARKER AND GLUE TO REST

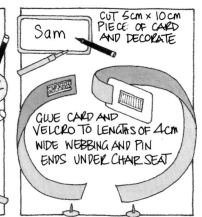

CUT 5cm × 10cm PIECE OF CARD AND DECORATE

Sam

GLUE CARD AND VELCRO TO LENGTHS OF 4cm WIDE WEBBING AND PIN ENDS UNDER CHAIR SEAT

Planet Balloons and Milky Way, and Shooting Star Garland

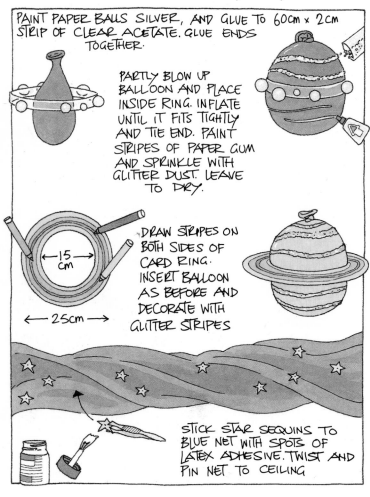

PAINT PAPER BALLS SILVER, AND GLUE TO 60cm × 2cm STRIP OF CLEAR ACETATE. GLUE ENDS TOGETHER.

PARTLY BLOW UP BALLOON AND PLACE INSIDE RING. INFLATE UNTIL IT FITS TIGHTLY AND TIE END. PAINT STRIPES OF PAPER GUM AND SPRINKLE WITH GLITTER DUST. LEAVE TO DRY.

15 cm

25cm

DRAW STRIPES ON BOTH SIDES OF CARD RING. INSERT BALLOON AS BEFORE AND DECORATE WITH GLITTER STRIPES

STICK STAR SEQUINS TO BLUE NET WITH SPOTS OF LATEX ADHESIVE. TWIST AND PIN NET TO CEILING

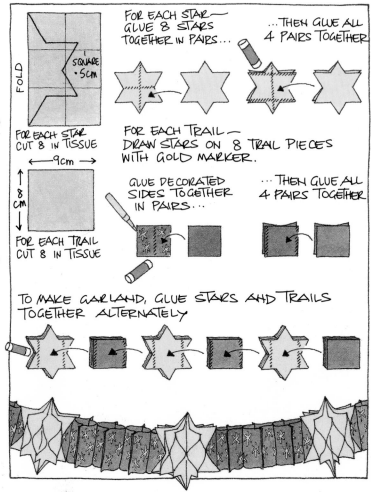

FOLD

1 SQUARE = 5cm

FOR EACH STAR CUT 8 IN TISSUE

9cm

8cm

FOR EACH TRAIL CUT 8 IN TISSUE

FOR EACH STAR GLUE 8 STARS TOGETHER IN PAIRS...

...THEN GLUE ALL 4 PAIRS TOGETHER

FOR EACH TRAIL DRAW STARS ON 8 TRAIL PIECES WITH GOLD MARKER.

GLUE DECORATED SIDES TOGETHER IN PAIRS...

...THEN GLUE ALL 4 PAIRS TOGETHER

TO MAKE GARLAND, GLUE STARS AND TRAILS TOGETHER ALTERNATELY

Spacewalkers and Whirling Comets

MEASURE SMALL TOY

HAND TO HAND →

↕ SHOULDER TO FEET

PAPER-BACKED FOIL

CUT OUT NECK HOLE

CUT UP CENTRE BACK

TAPE TOP OF BACK OPENING

MAKE CUTS, THEN WRAP PAPER ROUND ARMS AND LEGS, AND SECURE WITH STICKY TAPE. GLUE RIBBON ROUND WAIST

CUT OPENINGS IN OLD RUBBER BALL, AND PAINT SILVER

SEW STRONG THREAD TO HEAD AND THROUGH HELMET, AND SUSPEND TOY

GLUE FOIL WRAPPED MATCHBOX TO BACK

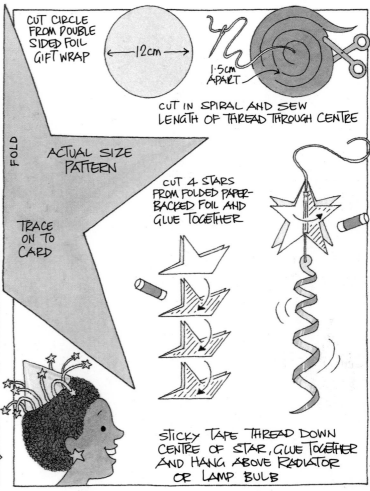

CUT CIRCLE FROM DOUBLE SIDED FOIL GIFT WRAP

12cm

1.5cm APART

CUT IN SPIRAL AND SEW LENGTH OF THREAD THROUGH CENTRE

FOLD

ACTUAL SIZE PATTERN

TRACE ON TO CARD

CUT 4 STARS FROM FOLDED PAPER-BACKED FOIL AND GLUE TOGETHER

STICKY TAPE THREAD DOWN CENTRE OF STAR, GLUE TOGETHER AND HANG ABOVE RADIATOR OR LAMP BULB

Crater Cloth, Lunar Plates, Galaxy Glasses, and Rocket Straws

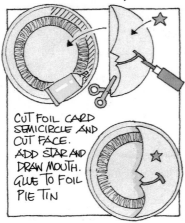

CAREFULLY SPRAY LARGE BUBBLE WRAP WITH COLOURED METALLIC CAR PAINTS

CUT FOIL CARD SEMICIRCLE AND CUT FACE. ADD STAR AND DRAW MOUTH. GLUE TO FOIL PIE TIN

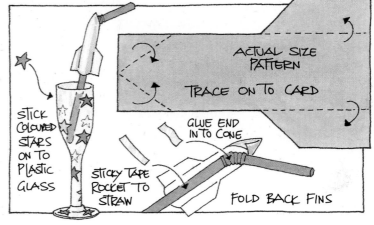

STICK COLOURED STARS ON TO PLASTIC GLASS

STICKY TAPE ROCKET TO STRAW

ACTUAL SIZE PATTERN

TRACE ON TO CARD

GLUE END IN TO CONE

FOLD BACK FINS

Fancy Dress

Astronaut

Shooting Star

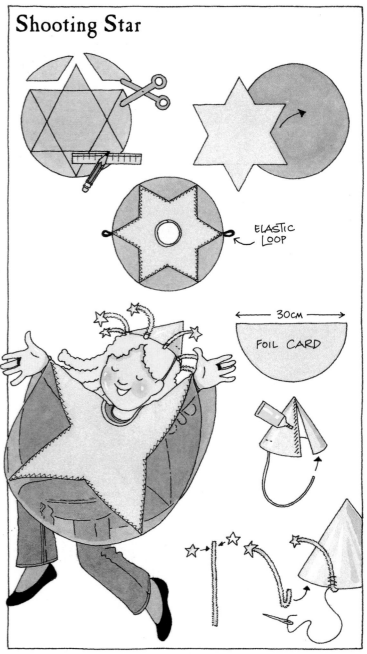

Make basic jacket and trousers in silver fabric, sewing metal zip down jacket front. Work 5 rows of shirring at elbows and knees, and elasticate sleeve and leg hems. Spray bathing cap and rubber gloves silver, and tape foil dishes to sides of cap. Wrap cardboard carton in foil and add webbing straps. Trim gumboots with foil sticky tape.

Cut paper circle to fit from hand to hand with arms outstretched. Mark six equal points round edge and join to make star pattern. Cut from lurex fabric and zig zag stitch to circle of sheer fabric. Cut out neck opening and bind. Glue card into cone and fit elastic strap. Sew lurex pipecleaners round brim and trim with merit stars.

Martian

Make basic mask and add paper ears. Cut 4 cups from an egg box and glue 2 together, inserting a pipecleaner in join. Glue to front of mask. Cut holes in the remaining cups and tape over eye holes in mask. Draw eyes with markers. Wear gloves and socks, and tack extra pair of padded gloves and socks under sleeve and trouser hems.

Saturnalia

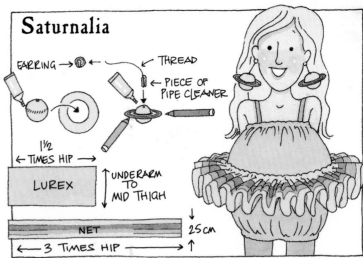

Join fabric to make a tube and elasticate top and bottom. Add ribbon straps and make leg holes by catching base with a few stitches. Wind wadding round body to pad costume. Sew net strips together, and make as for basic skirt, adjusting elastic to fit. Cut card rings to fit beads, then glue in place and colour. Fix to earrings.

Rocket

Cut basic trouser pattern down outside leg, add turnings and cut from fabric. Sew fin pieces together in pairs, turn to right side and insert in seam. Complete trousers and catch strips of net round hems with a few stitches. Make sleeveless basic jacket, adding sequins and felt numbers. Glue card into cone and fix elastic chin strap.

Man in the Moon

Inflate large round balloon until slightly bigger than head. Cover with two layers of newspaper, soaked in wallpaper paste. Glue egg box cup 'craters' in place and cover with another two layers of paper. Leave to dry, burst balloon, then cut face and neck hole. Paint moon and wear with sequin-decorated tee shirt and trousers.

Food and Drink

Unidentified Flying Sandwiches

CUT ROUND ROLL IN HALF. BUTTER AND SPREAD FILLING ON BOTH SIDES

CUT CIRCLE OF COLD TOAST AND PLACE BETWEEN ROLL

SAUCER

DECORATE WITH SWEETCORN

PUSH A TOAST TRIANGLE INTO EACH SIDE

DECORATE WITH PUMPKIN SEEDS

CUT LONG ROLL IN HALF AND SPREAD WITH FILLING

Moon Rocks

BRING 150 ML WATER, PINCH OF SALT AND 50G BUTTER TO THE BOIL

REMOVE FROM THE HEAT AND QUICKLY STIR IN 60G PLAIN FLOUR — THEN MIX IN 2 BEATEN EGGS

PLACE TEASPOONS OF MIXTURE ON GREASED TRAYS, SPRINKLE WITH POPPY SEEDS AND BAKE FOR 10 MINUTES AT 425°F/220°C/GAS MARK 7

LEAVE TO COOL ON RACK, PIERCE EACH ROCK WITH KNIFE AND FILL WITH CREAM CHEESE MIXTURE

Cosmic Cookies

MAKE DOUBLE QUANTITY OF BASIC BISCUIT DOUGH AND DIVIDE INTO FOUR PIECES

KNEAD IN

2 TEASPOONS COCOA POWDER

50G CHOPPED CHERRIES

50G CHOPPED NUTS

50G CURRANTS

ROLL OUT, CUT WITH 6 CM WIDE STAR CUTTER AND BAKE

SPREAD SOME WITH GLACÉ ICING, HALF DIP SOME IN MELTED CHOCOLATE AND, SANDWICH SOME TOGETHER WITH BUTTER CREAM

Multicoloured Meteors

MELT 110g PLAIN CHOCOLATE AND 10g BUTTER IN BASIN OVER HOT WATER

REMOVE FROM HEAT AND STIR IN 110g ICING SUGAR, 1 EGG YOLK, AND 110g SIEVED CAKE CRUMBS

FORM INTO SMALL BALLS, THEN ROLL IN COLOURED SPRINKLES AND LEAVE TO SET

ALBERT— YOU'D BETTER HIDE THESE UNTIL THE PARTY!

Planet Punch

BLEND TOGETHER —
200 ML CREAM SODA
300g NATURAL YOGURT
275 ML VANILLA ICE CREAM

ADD A FEW DROPS OF PEPPERMINT FLAVOURING TO TASTE, AND TINT PALE BLUE WITH FOOD COLOURING

QUARTER FILL GLASSES WITH MIXTURE AND TOP UP WITH CREAM SODA

WE'LL NEED PLENTY OF THESE FOR THE FLIGHT TO THE MOON, MUM!

Sparkling Spaceship

FIX LARGE AND EXTRA LARGE SWISS ROLLS TOGETHER WITH BUTTER CREAM

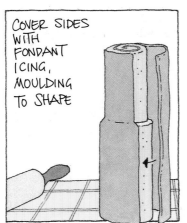
COVER SIDES WITH FONDANT ICING, MOULDING TO SHAPE

FIX COLOURED ICE CREAM CONE TO TOP AND 4 CONE STEMS TO BASE

DECORATE WITH JELLY SWEETS AND INDOOR SPARKLERS. LIGHT CAREFULLY WHEN READY

Games

Moonrock Grab

Groups of three players are each given a 3 metre length of rope, knotted to make a band. Players form a triangle and hold the rope taut with their left hands. Screwed up pieces of kitchen foil are placed on the floor, out of reach of the players. The first person to pick up their moonrock without letting go of the rope is the winner.

Lost in Space!

Arrange several cushions over the floor and scatter ten toy squeakers, bought from a haberdashery shop, on and between the cushions. Cover with a duvet and line up all the players at one end. Each player takes it in turn to walk blindfolded over the duvet. If they happen to tread on a squeaking alien they must return and start again.

Stellar Pebbles

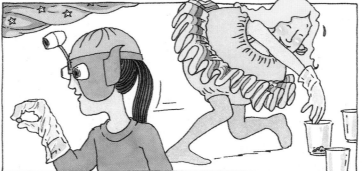

Line up players at one side of the room and give each one a disposable plastic glove and a saucer. On the opposite side of the room place a tumbler, holding ten pieces of puffed rice cereal, for each person. The players run and pick up one pebble with a gloved hand, then take it back to their saucer. The first with a full saucer wins.

CHAPTER 9

Prehistoric Party

Decorations

Dinosaur and Painted Rock Invitations, and Ammonite Rings

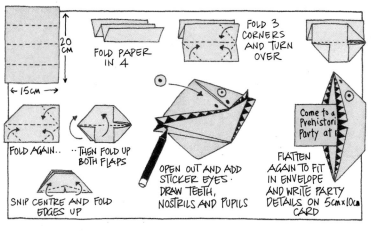

20 CM

15 CM

FOLD PAPER IN 4

FOLD 3 CORNERS AND TURN OVER

FOLD AGAIN..

..THEN FOLD UP BOTH FLAPS

SNIP CENTRE AND FOLD EDGES UP

OPEN OUT AND ADD STICKER EYES. DRAW TEETH, NOSTRILS AND PUPILS

FLATTEN AGAIN TO FIT IN ENVELOPE AND WRITE PARTY DETAILS ON 5cm x 10cm CARD

Come to a Prehistoric Party at...

BREAK PIECE FROM POLYSTYRENE TILE AND DRAW OUTLINE OF ANIMAL WITH PERMANENT MARKER

COLOUR WITH MARKERS, BLOT AND LEAVE TO DRY. WRITE DETAILS ON BACK

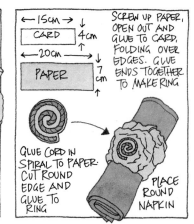

15 CM
CARD
4 CM

20 CM
PAPER
7 CM

SCREW UP PAPER, OPEN OUT AND GLUE TO CARD, FOLDING OVER EDGES. GLUE ENDS TOGETHER TO MAKING RING

GLUE CORD IN SPIRAL TO PAPER. CUT ROUND EDGE AND GLUE TO RING

PLACE ROUND NAPKIN

Cave Walls, Blazing Torches, and Primeval Forest Trees

DRAW ON SHEETS OF BROWN WRAPPING PAPER...

...THEN SCREW THEM UP...

...OPEN OUT AND PIN OVER WALL

50 CM

PAPER-BACKED FOIL

GLUE INTO CONE AND INSERT BALL OF TISSUE

GATHER BASE AND SECURE WITH STICKY TAPE

15 CM

25 CM
CORRUGATED CARD

GENTLY TWIST INTO SPIRAL

WIND CARD ROUND BASE OF FLAME AND GLUE

40 CM

15 CM
BROWN PAPER

FOLD IN HALF AND FRINGE. OPEN OUT AND WIND ROUND BASE OF FLAME

BIND WITH COARSE STRING

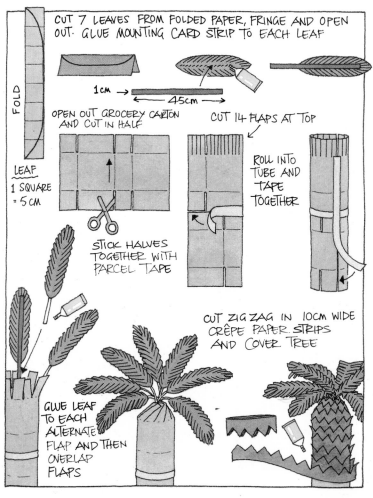

FOLD

LEAF
1 SQUARE = 5 CM

CUT 7 LEAVES FROM FOLDED PAPER, FRINGE AND OPEN OUT. GLUE MOUNTING CARD STRIP TO EACH LEAF

1 CM
45 CM

OPEN OUT GROCERY CARTON AND CUT IN HALF

STICK HALVES TOGETHER WITH PARCEL TAPE

CUT 14 FLAPS AT TOP

ROLL INTO TUBE AND TAPE TOGETHER

CUT ZIG ZAG IN 10CM WIDE CRÊPE PAPER STRIPS AND COVER TREE

GLUE LEAF TO EACH ALTERNATE FLAP AND THEN OVERLAP FLAPS

Pterodactyl Garland and Thonged Skin Tablecloth

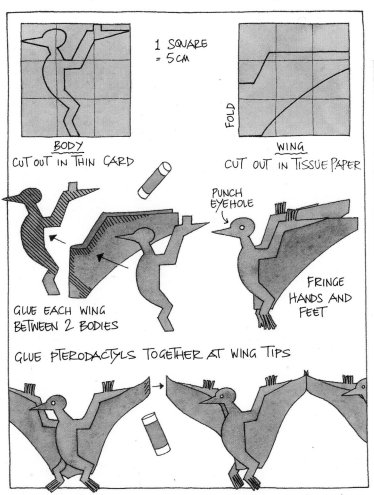

1 SQUARE = 5 CM

FOLD

BODY
CUT OUT IN THIN CARD

WING
CUT OUT IN TISSUE PAPER

PUNCH EYEHOLE

GLUE EACH WING BETWEEN 2 BODIES

FRINGE HANDS AND FEET

GLUE PTERODACTYLS TOGETHER AT WING TIPS

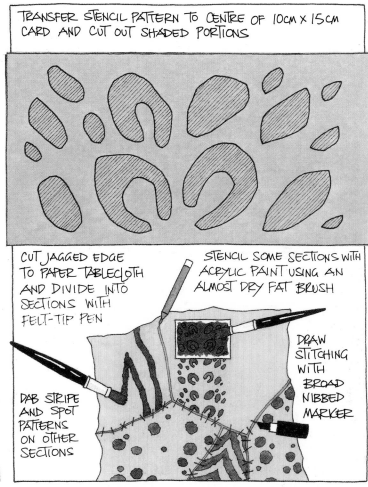

TRANSFER STENCIL PATTERN TO CENTRE OF 10CM × 15CM CARD AND CUT OUT SHADED PORTIONS

CUT JAGGED EDGE TO PAPER TABLECLOTH AND DIVIDE INTO SECTIONS WITH FELT-TIP PEN

STENCIL SOME SECTIONS WITH ACRYLIC PAINT USING AN ALMOST DRY FAT BRUSH

DRAW STITCHING WITH BROAD NIBBED MARKER

DAB STRIPE AND SPOT PATTERNS ON OTHER SECTIONS

Bone Cutlery, Fossil Plates, and Spear Straws

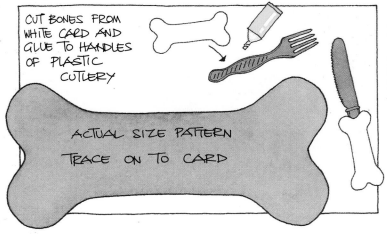

CUT BONES FROM WHITE CARD AND GLUE TO HANDLES OF PLASTIC CUTLERY

ACTUAL SIZE PATTERN

TRACE ON TO CARD

PLACE FERNS ON BLACK PAPER PLATE AND SPRAY WITH GREY PRIMER

REMOVE FERNS AND LEAVE PLATE TO DRY

CUT POINT FROM CARD AND STICK TO STRAW WITH TAPE

ACTUAL SIZE PATTERN

TRACE ON TO CARD

BIND WITH STRING

Fancy Dress

Brontosaurus

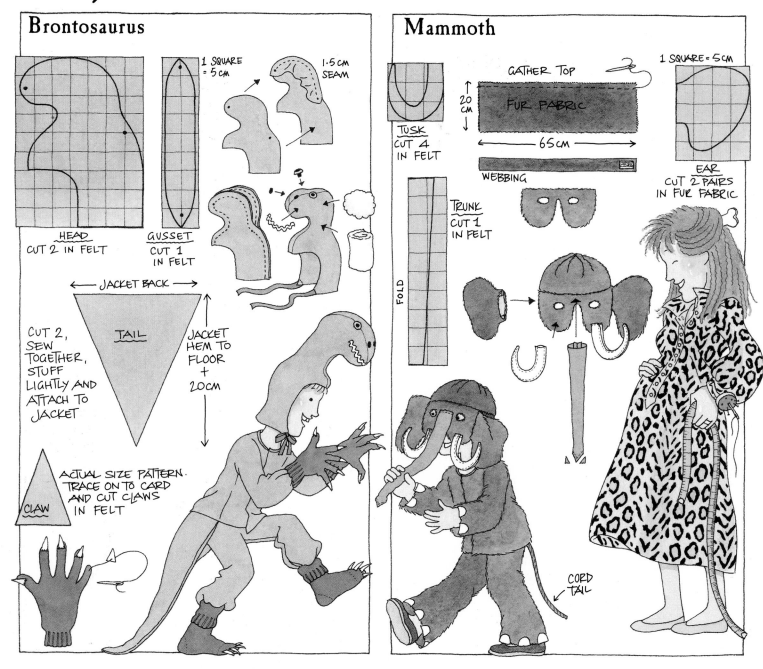

1 SQUARE = 5 CM

1.5 CM SEAM

HEAD
CUT 2 IN FELT

GUSSET
CUT 1 IN FELT

JACKET BACK

TAIL

CUT 2, SEW TOGETHER, STUFF LIGHTLY AND ATTACH TO JACKET

JACKET HEM TO FLOOR + 20CM

CLAW

ACTUAL SIZE PATTERN. TRACE ON TO CARD AND CUT CLAWS IN FELT

Mammoth

GATHER TOP

20 CM

FUR FABRIC

65CM

WEBBING

1 SQUARE = 5CM

TUSK
CUT 4 IN FELT

TRUNK
CUT 1 IN FELT

FOLD

EAR
CUT 2 PAIRS IN FUR FABRIC

CORD TAIL

Sew gusset to one head piece between marks, then sew head pieces together. Turn to right side and fix eyes. Stuff head and insert rolled piece of wadding in neck. Decorate with braid and felt, and add tape ties. Make basic jacket and trousers and sew tail to back of jacket. Cut felt triangle claws and sew to thick socks and woollen gloves.

Cover face section of basic mask with fur fabric. Join ear pieces and sew to mask sides. Join trunk seam, stuff, sew across end and sew to mask. Sew tusk pieces together, stuff, and sew to mask. Complete mask by sewing together, and join with Velcro. Make basic jacket and trousers, sew felt semicircles round sleeve and leg hems, and add tail.

Stone Age Hunter

Cut rectangle of fabric diagonally to make one-shouldered costume. Cover with oddments of fur fabric, tacking in place and overlapping edges. Work a zig zag stitch over raw edges and remove tacking. Sew side seams and tie rope round waist. Tape balloon to end of card tube and cover with crumpled newspaper soaked in paste. Paint when dry.

Triceratops

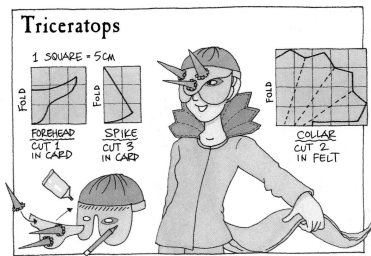

Make brontosaurus jacket and trousers. Sew collar pieces together close to cut edge, leaving base open. Insert wadding and quilt along marked lines, then sew to jacket neck. Cut tabs along top edge of forehead piece and glue to basic mask. Glue horn pieces into cones, then cut tabs round base and glue in place. Draw eyes with felt pen.

Stegosaurus

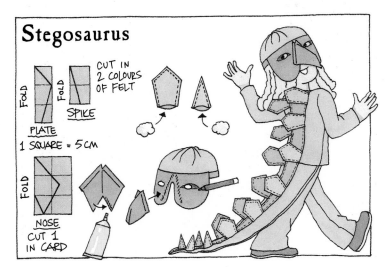

Make jacket and trousers as for brontosaurus. Cut a strip of felt to fit across back neck, tapering down to base of tail, and sew to jacket. Sew plate pieces together, leaving base open, and stuff lightly. Repeat for spikes and sew down sides of felt strip. Glue base dart on nose piece, then glue to basic mask and draw eyes with pens.

Cavewoman

Make tabard from hessian rectangle, cutting hole for neck opening. Join side seams and tie a strip of fur fabric round waist. Cut bone and teeth from a polystyrene tile, using a craft knife. Thread teeth on to twine and tie round neck. Wind hair round bone and fasten with a hairpin. Glue strips of fur fabric round plastic bangles.

Food and Drink

Brushwood Fires

HERE'S SOME FOOD WE CAN MAKE BETWEEN US, DAISY!

SPREAD CRACKER WITH BUTTER, THEN TOP WITH DOLLOP OF CREAM CHEESE

SURROUND WITH SAVOURY COCKTAIL TWIGS

PUSH ORANGE PEPPER AND CHEESE TRIANGLE FLAMES INTO CREAM CHEESE

I DON'T THINK THE BRONTOSAURUS LIKES CREAM CHEESE

I THINK HE DOES!

Tyrannosaur's Jaws

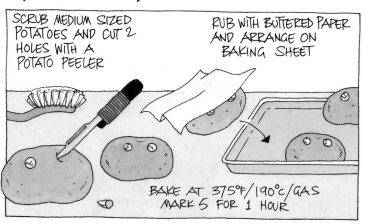

SCRUB MEDIUM SIZED POTATOES AND CUT 2 HOLES WITH A POTATO PEELER

RUB WITH BUTTERED PAPER AND ARRANGE ON BAKING SHEET

BAKE AT 375°F/190°C/GAS MARK 5 FOR 1 HOUR

CUT ZIGZAG ALONG EACH POTATO AND PRESS ENDS TO OPEN JAWS

PUSH STUFFED OLIVES INTO EYE HOLES

SERVE WITH BUTTER AND A SELECTION OF BASIC SANDWICH FILLINGS

Erupting Volcanoes

RUB TOGETHER — 350g PLAIN FLOUR, 2 TEASPOONS BAKING POWDER, ½ TEASPOON MIXED SPICE, 175g BROWN SUGAR, AND 175g BUTTER

MIX IN A BEATEN EGG AND 2 TABLESPOONS MILK··THEN STIR IN 75g CURRANTS AND 25g MIXED PEEL

MAKE SMALL PYRAMIDS OF THE MIXTURE ON GREASED BAKING SHEETS, AND MAKE HOLE IN CENTRE

BAKE AT 375°F/190°C/GAS MARK 5 FOR 20 MINUTES

LEAVE TO COOL AND FILL HOLES WITH WARMED JAM

Dinosaur Lollies

COME ON, BRIAN! IT'S TIME YOU DID SOME COOKING!

OK, CHRISTINE! FIRST CUT BANANAS IN HALF. PUSH ON TO LOLLIPOP STICK AND FREEZE FOR 1 HOUR

DIP INTO MELTED CHOCOLATE AND PRESS IN FLAKED ALMONDS AND JELLY SWEETS BEFORE CHOCOLATE SETS

RETURN TO FREEZER AND REMOVE 10 MINUTES BEFORE SERVING

Swamp Fizz

POUR 1 LITRE CHOCOLATE MILK INTO ICE CUBE TRAYS AND FREEZE

MIX TOGETHER ½ LITRE CHOCOLATE ICE CREAM AND 4 TABLESPOONS MILK TO MAKE A THICK MILKSHAKE

CRUSH CHOCOLATE ICE CUBES IN A PLASTIC BAG, HALF FILL GLASSES AND TOP UP WITH FIZZY ORANGEADE

TOP WITH A TABLESPOON OF MILKSHAKE AND DUST WITH DRINKING CHOCOLATE

Cave Cake

MAKE BASIC PARTY CAKE MIXTURE, COLOUR HALF PINK AND PUT BOTH HALVES IN A GREASED OVENPROOF 1 LITRE BASIN, SWIRLING COLOURS TOGETHER WITH A SKEWER

BAKE FOR 1 HOUR AT 325°F/170°C/GAS MARK 3 AND LEAVE TO COOL

SPREAD CAKE WITH JAM AND COVER WITH HALVED MINI DOUGHNUTS

MAKE TREES FROM MINI CHOCOLATE SWISS ROLLS AND JELLY SWEETS ON COCKTAIL STICKS

CUT OUT CAVE OPENING

ADD DINOSAUR TOYS

Games

Dinosaur Tracks

Cut two paper dinosaur footprints for each player. The players stand in line at one end of the room and are given their footprints to stand on – one under each foot.

At the word 'Go!' they shuffle across the room, keeping the footprints under their feet. If anyone touches the floor with their feet they must return to the beginning.

Weirdosaurus!

Each person is given a sheet of paper and told to draw a monster's head at the top. They then fold down the top of the paper to hide the head, and pass the sheet to the

next player. The body, legs, and feet are then drawn in turn, folding and passing on the paper as before. Names are invented for the monsters when the sheets are opened.

Swamp or Lava?

Tear small islands from paper, one for each player. Draw a volcano on one island, and scatter them over the floor. As the music starts, the players walk in a circle, and

when it stops they must each stand on an island. Whoever is standing on the volcano drops out, as does anyone left in the 'swamp'. One island is removed after each round.

CHAPTER 10

Spooky Party

Decorations

Ghost and Witch Invitations, and Spider Balloons

CUT GHOST FROM PAPER, DECORATE AND GLUE THROUGH 1CM WIDE SLOT ON FRONT OF FOLDED CARD

8CM
10 CM
15CM

FOLD

1 SQUARE = 5CM

DRAW HAT, SCARF AND FEATURES ON 10CM x 15CM FOLDED CARD

GLUE ON STRAND FROM FRINGING FOR PROFILE AND PIECE OF FRINGE FOR HAIR. WRITE PARTY DETAILS INSIDE CARD

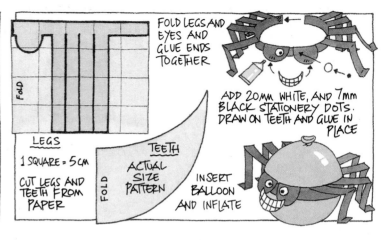

FOLD LEGS AND EYES AND GLUE ENDS TOGETHER

ADD 20MM WHITE, AND 7MM BLACK STATIONERY DOTS. DRAW ON TEETH AND GLUE IN PLACE

FOLD

LEGS
1 SQUARE = 5CM
CUT LEGS AND TEETH FROM PAPER

TEETH
ACTUAL SIZE PATTERN

FOLD

INSERT BALLOON AND INFLATE

Pumpkin Patch Garland and Hovering Bats

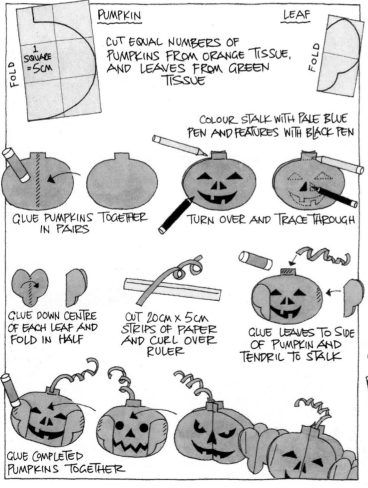

PUMPKIN

1 SQUARE = 5CM

LEAF

FOLD

CUT EQUAL NUMBERS OF PUMPKINS FROM ORANGE TISSUE, AND LEAVES FROM GREEN TISSUE

COLOUR STALK WITH PALE BLUE PEN AND FEATURES WITH BLACK PEN

GLUE PUMPKINS TOGETHER IN PAIRS

TURN OVER AND TRACE THROUGH

GLUE DOWN CENTRE OF EACH LEAF AND FOLD IN HALF

CUT 20CM x 5CM STRIPS OF PAPER AND CURL OVER RULER

GLUE LEAVES TO SIDE OF PUMPKIN AND TENDRIL TO STALK

GLUE COMPLETED PUMPKINS TOGETHER

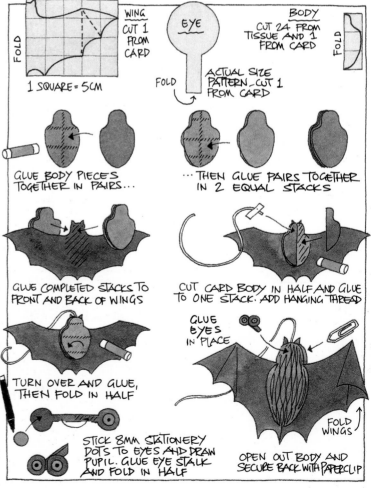

FOLD

WING
CUT 1 FROM CARD

EYE

BODY
CUT 24 FROM TISSUE AND 1 FROM CARD

FOLD

1 SQUARE = 5CM

FOLD

ACTUAL SIZE PATTERN_CUT 1 FROM CARD

GLUE BODY PIECES TOGETHER IN PAIRS...

...THEN GLUE PAIRS TOGETHER IN 2 EQUAL STACKS

GLUE COMPLETED STACKS TO FRONT AND BACK OF WINGS

CUT CARD BODY IN HALF AND GLUE TO ONE STACK. ADD HANGING THREAD

TURN OVER AND GLUE, THEN FOLD IN HALF

GLUE EYES IN PLACE

STICK 8MM STATIONERY DOTS TO EYES AND DRAW PUPIL. GLUE EYE STALK AND FOLD IN HALF

OPEN OUT BODY AND SECURE BACK WITH PAPERCLIP

FOLD WINGS

Skull Lanterns, Tombstone Chairs, and Phantom Markers

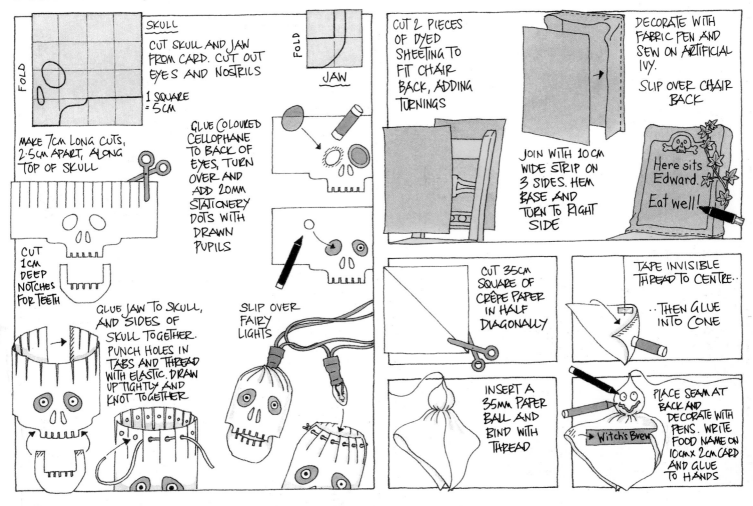

SKULL
CUT SKULL AND JAW FROM CARD. CUT OUT EYES AND NOSTRILS

FOLD

JAW

1 SQUARE = 5CM

MAKE 7cm LONG CUTS, 2.5cm APART, ALONG TOP OF SKULL

GLUE COLOURED CELLOPHANE TO BACK OF EYES, TURN OVER AND ADD 20MM STATIONERY DOTS WITH DRAWN PUPILS

CUT 1CM DEEP NOTCHES FOR TEETH

GLUE JAW TO SKULL, AND SIDES OF SKULL TOGETHER. PUNCH HOLES IN TABS AND THREAD WITH ELASTIC. DRAW UP TIGHTLY AND KNOT TOGETHER

SLIP OVER FAIRY LIGHTS

CUT 2 PIECES OF DYED SHEETING TO FIT CHAIR BACK, ADDING TURNINGS

JOIN WITH 10CM WIDE STRIP ON 3 SIDES. HEM BASE AND TURN TO RIGHT SIDE

DECORATE WITH FABRIC PEN AND SEW ON ARTIFICIAL IVY.
SLIP OVER CHAIR BACK

Here sits Edward.
Eat well!

CUT 35CM SQUARE OF CRÊPE PAPER IN HALF DIAGONALLY

INSERT A 35MM PAPER BALL AND BIND WITH THREAD

TAPE INVISIBLE THREAD TO CENTRE...
...THEN GLUE INTO CONE

Witch's Brew

PLACE SEAM AT BACK AND DECORATE WITH PENS. WRITE FOOD NAME ON 10CM x 2CM CARD AND GLUE TO HANDS

Ghost Cups, Spider Straws, Pumpkin Plates, and Bat Napkins

ACTUAL SIZE PATTERN

CUT OUT FROM CARD, FOLD AND GLUE TO PAPER CUP. ADD 15MM STATIONERY DOTS FOR EYES AND DRAW MOUTH

CUT PIPECLEANER IN QUARTERS, BEND IN HALF AND GLUE TO 30CM CARD CIRCLE

DECORATE WITH POSTER PAINT AND 5MM JOGGLE EYES, AND TAPE TO STRAW

1 SQUARE = 5CM

FOLD

MOUTH

EYES & NOSE

CUT FEATURES FROM SELF-ADHESIVE PLASTIC. CUT OUT TEETH, REMOVE BACKING AND STICK TO PAPER PLATE

CUT BAT FROM FOLDED CARD AND GLUE HEADS TOGETHER.
DECORATE WITH HALVED 15MM STATIONERY DOT AND PEN

FOLD 1 SQUARE = 5CM

INSERT FOLDED NAPKIN

Fancy Dress

Witches

EYE STENCIL

FOLD

ACTUAL SIZE PATTERN
CUT FROM CARD

SKULL STENCIL

ACTUAL SIZE PATTERN CUT FROM CARD

←FOLD

CUT 2 FELT
1 SQUARE = 5CM
NOSE

HIP

CLOAK

SHOULDER TO HEM + 15CM

40cm

40 CM

HAT CROWN
CUT 1 FELT

HAT BRIM
←45CM→
CUT 1 FELT

2 BASIC SKIRTS

Jack O'Lantern

1 SQUARE = 5CM

LEAF

FOLD

NOSE
CUT 1 FROM CARD

CUT 6 FROM FELT

⅛ HIP

BODY
CUT 8

UNDERARM TO KNEE

¼ HIP

⅛ HIP

Sew hat into cone, adjusting to fit. Cut hole in brim to fit and oversew edges together. Glue yarn or paper fringe hair inside hat. Hem cloak, then sew tape 10cm down from top and thread with cord. Oversew nose pieces, turn to other side, stuff tip and add elastic. Stencil clothes with fabric paint, adding fabric pen or sequin features.

Stitch body pieces together, then elasticate top and bottom to fit and add tape straps. Wear over polo-necked sweater, padding waist with wadding. Make basic mask, binding top on right side to make stalk, and add leaf. Colour eyes and glue on nose triangle. Sew felt leaves round neck and trim shoes with bobble and felt pumpkins.

Bat

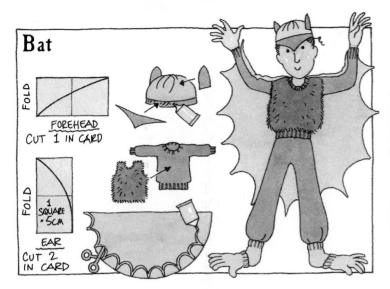

Cut semicircle of satin to fit from wrist to wrist with outstretched arms, and cut scallops round edge, using the basic non-fray glue method. Cut fur fabric to fit front of sweater and tack in place, then sew wings to sweater sleeves. Make top portion of basic mask and add card ears and forehead. Sew woollen gloves to toes of thick socks.

Skeleton

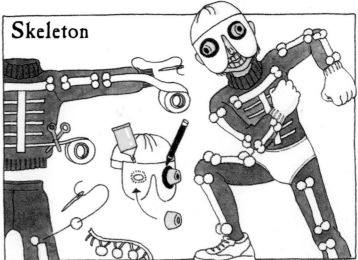

Sew white cotton tape to black sweater and thick tights, and stitch small bobbles cut from lampshade fringing in place to make joints. Wear with white briefs and gloves. Make basic mask in white and colour eye sockets black. Cut eye holes from egg box cups and tape in place. Draw nose holes and teeth on face with black eyebrow pencil.

Devil

Cover wide hairband with felt. Oversew horns to make cones, stuff and sew to hairband. Cut beard and eyebrows from fur fabric and fix to face with eyelash glue. Draw widow's peak with eyebrow pencil. Make tail from thick cord and card and sew to back of trousers. Sew curved strips of felt round trouser hems to make cloven feet.

Ghost

Drape with old sheet and trim base if needed. Mark and cut eye holes, place over a piece of blue net and zig zag stitch round cut edges, then trim away excess net at back. Draw mouth with red fabric paint pen. Catch sides of costume together to form wrist openings, and carry a candelabra which has been draped with angel hair cobwebs.

Food and Drink

Pumpkin Pizzas

USING 550g PACKET MIX, MAKE BREAD DOUGH. DIVIDE INTO 16 PIECES, ROLL OUT INTO 10CM CIRCLES AND PLACE ON BUTTERED TRAYS

SPREAD WITH A LITTLE TOMATO SAUCE AND SAUTÉED ONIONS. SPRINKLE WITH OREGANO AND SEASON

TOP WITH THIN SLICES OF CHEDDAR CHEESE AND DECORATE WITH PIECES OF PEPPER

BAKE AT 408°F / 200°C / GAS MARK 6 FOR 15 MINUTES AND SERVE IMMEDIATELY

Skull and Spider Savouries

BUTTER SLICES FROM A ROUND LOAF, THEN SPREAD HALF WITH TOMATO CHEESE FILLING

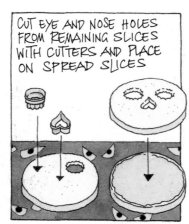

CUT EYE AND NOSE HOLES FROM REMAINING SLICES WITH CUTTERS AND PLACE ON SPREAD SLICES

PRESS HALF COCKTAIL ONIONS AND OLIVE SLIVERS INTO EYE HOLES

TRIM WITH CUTTER AND MARK MOUTH WITH PASTRY WHEEL

SANDWICH BROWN FRENCH LOAF SLICES WITH COTTAGE CHEESE AND CUT EYE HOLES

PUSH IN 8 SAVOURY TWIG LEGS AND CURRANT EYES. DRAW MOUTH WITH TOMATO PASTE

Bewitching Bats

MAKE BASIC BISCUIT DOUGH, ADDING 1 TABLESPOON COCOA POWDER, AND ROLL OUT

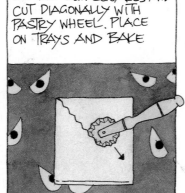

CUT INTO 5CM SQUARES AND CUT DIAGONALLY WITH PASTRY WHEEL. PLACE ON TRAYS AND BAKE

CUT SLITS AND GENTLY PUSH WINGS INTO SIDES OF CHOCOLATE TRUFFLES

ADD FEATURES WITH ICING AND COLOURED DRAGEES

WHO'S THAT?

I DON'T KNOW, BUT IT'S GOT MY BAT!

Hallowe'en Hats

TRIM 8 ICE CREAM CONES, BRUSH WITH MELTED CHOCOLATE AND LEAVE TO SET

STIR 4 EGG YOLKS INTO 150g MELTED WHITE CHOCOLATE, THEN ADD A FEW DROPS OF GREEN COLOURING AND PEPPERMINT ESSENCE

FOLD 4 WHISKED EGG WHITES INTO MIXTURE. STAND CONES IN BASIN PACKED WITH KITCHEN PAPER, FILL WITH MIXTURE AND REFRIGERATE TO SET

FIX TO CHOCOLATE COVERED BISCUITS WITH A LITTLE MELTED CHOCOLATE. ADD BANDS OF FONDANT ICING

Witch's Brew

PLACE SCOOPS OF RIPPLE ICE CREAM ON TRAY LINED WITH WAXED PAPER

QUICKLY DRAW FEATURES WITH SYRUPS AND FREEZE TO SET

ALMOST FILL CUPS WITH COLA DRINK, PIPE WHIPPED CREAM ROUND RIM AND TOP WITH ICE CREAM GHOST

I DON'T COOK JUST FOR GHOSTS, YOU KNOW!

Skeleton Sponge

CUT 2 LARGE AND 1 MINI CHOCOLATE COVERED SWISS ROLLS AS SHOWN

EAT THIS HALF!

BRUSH MELTED CHOCOLATE ON CUT ENDS

ADD 10 MORE MINI ROLLS

FIX TO BOARD WITH ICING AND PIPE BONES WITH REMAINING ICING

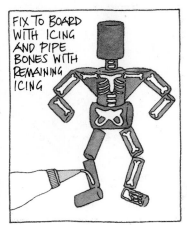

1 SQUARE = 5CM

FOLD

CUT SKULL AND HANDS FROM FONDANT ICING AND FIX IN PLACE

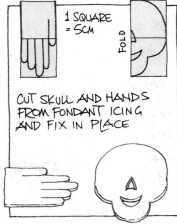

FIX CHOCOLATE EYEBALLS IN PLACE AND ICE FEATURES

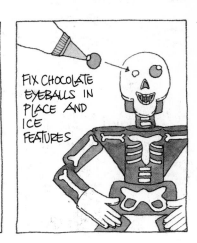

Games

Sleepy Vampires

Clear a large space of furniture and any rugs that could be tripped over. The players all lie on the floor with arms crossed. As soon as the lights are turned off they awake and roam about, making blood-curdling noises. When the lights are turned on they must return to their tombs, and the last vampire to lie down drops out of the game.

Catchee Spider

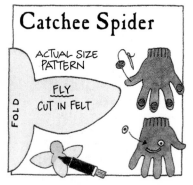

Using the hook side, sew five Velcro spots to a woollen glove, adding toy eyes and felt mouth. Cut 20 flies from felt and colour with fabric pen. Cover the top of a deep carton with fabric and cut a slit in the centre. Drop the flies in the box and give each player 5 seconds to catch them with the spider glove, scoring 5 points for each fly.

Wail, Ghost!

One player is given a cushion and blindfolded, and then turned round three times. All the other people sit in a circle. The blind man finds a player, places the cushion on their lap and sits on it. He then says 'Wail, ghost', and the person he is sitting on makes a spooky sound. If the blind man recognises the player they change places.

CHAPTER 11

Christmas Party

Decorations

Tree and Gift Invitations, and Cone Gnome Place Marker

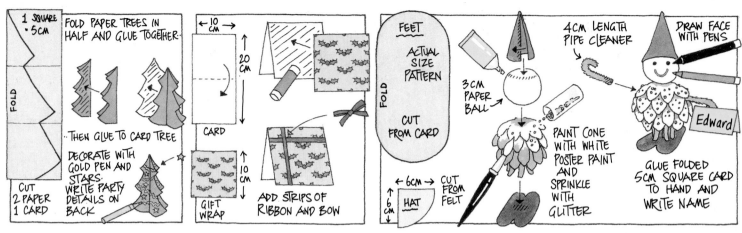

1 SQUARE = 5CM

FOLD

FOLD PAPER TREES IN HALF AND GLUE TOGETHER.

...THEN GLUE TO CARD TREE

DECORATE WITH GOLD PEN AND STARS. WRITE PARTY DETAILS ON BACK

CUT 2 PAPER 1 CARD

← 10 CM →

20 CM

CARD

10 CM

GIFT WRAP

ADD STRIPS OF RIBBON AND BOW

FEET

FOLD

ACTUAL SIZE PATTERN

CUT FROM CARD

← 6CM → CUT FROM FELT

6 CM

HAT

4CM LENGTH PIPE CLEANER

3CM PAPER BALL

PAINT CONE WITH WHITE POSTER PAINT AND SPRINKLE WITH GLITTER

DRAW FACE WITH PENS

Edward

GLUE FOLDED 5CM SQUARE CARD TO HAND AND WRITE NAME

Holly and Mistletoe Garlands, Snowball Icelights, and Icicles

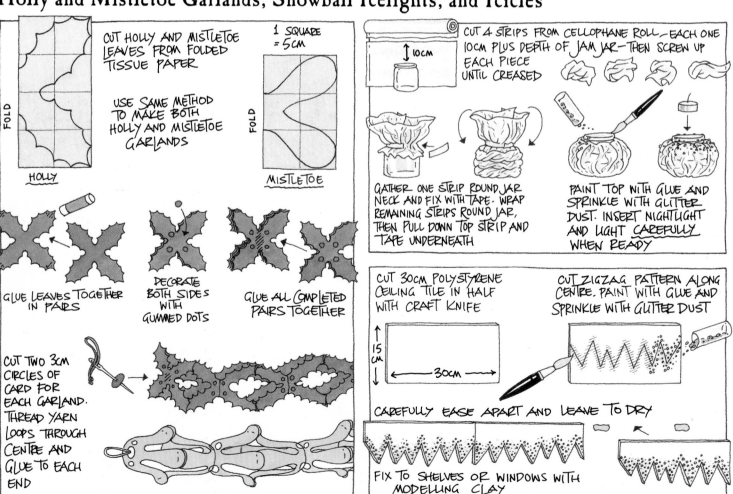

CUT HOLLY AND MISTLETOE LEAVES FROM FOLDED TISSUE PAPER

USE SAME METHOD TO MAKE BOTH HOLLY AND MISTLETOE GARLANDS

FOLD

HOLLY

1 SQUARE = 5CM

FOLD

MISTLETOE

GLUE LEAVES TOGETHER IN PAIRS

DECORATE BOTH SIDES WITH GUMMED DOTS

GLUE ALL COMPLETED PAIRS TOGETHER

CUT TWO 3CM CIRCLES OF CARD FOR EACH GARLAND. THREAD YARN LOOPS THROUGH CENTRE AND GLUE TO EACH END

10CM

CUT 4 STRIPS FROM CELLOPHANE ROLL—EACH ONE 10CM PLUS DEPTH OF JAM JAR—THEN SCREW UP EACH PIECE UNTIL CREASED

GATHER ONE STRIP ROUND JAR NECK AND FIX WITH TAPE. WRAP REMAINING STRIPS ROUND JAR, THEN PULL DOWN TOP STRIP AND TAPE UNDERNEATH

PAINT TOP WITH GLUE AND SPRINKLE WITH GLITTER DUST. INSERT NIGHTLIGHT AND LIGHT CAREFULLY WHEN READY

CUT 30CM POLYSTYRENE CEILING TILE IN HALF WITH CRAFT KNIFE

CUT ZIGZAG PATTERN ALONG CENTRE. PAINT WITH GLUE AND SPRINKLE WITH GLITTER DUST

15 CM

← 30CM →

CAREFULLY EASE APART AND LEAVE TO DRY

FIX TO SHELVES OR WINDOWS WITH MODELLING CLAY

Victorian Santa and Cherub Trims, and Snowscene Tree Skirt

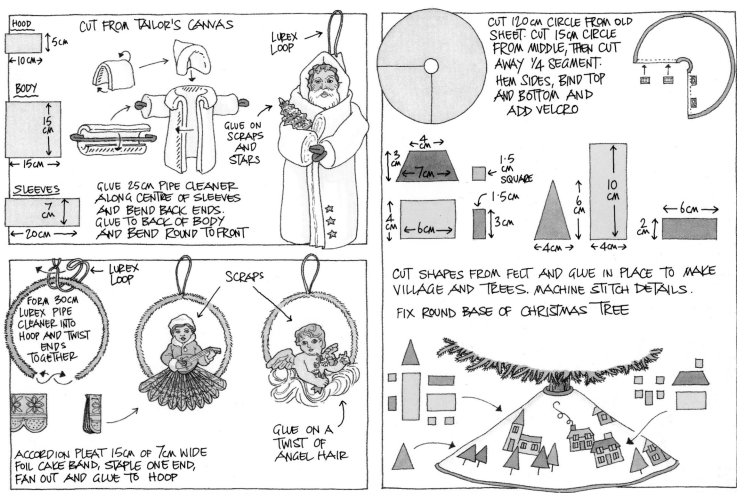

HOOD
↕5CM
←10CM→

CUT FROM TAILOR'S CANVAS

LUREX LOOP

BODY
↕15 CM
←15CM→

GLUE ON SCRAPS AND STARS

SLEEVES
↕7 CM
←20CM→

GLUE 25CM PIPE CLEANER ALONG CENTRE OF SLEEVES AND BEND BACK ENDS. GLUE TO BACK OF BODY AND BEND ROUND TO FRONT

CUT 120CM CIRCLE FROM OLD SHEET. CUT 15CM CIRCLE FROM MIDDLE, THEN CUT AWAY ¼ SEGMENT. HEM SIDES, BIND TOP AND BOTTOM AND ADD VELCRO

←4CM→
↕3CM
←7CM→

1·5 CM SQUARE

1·5CM
↕3CM

↕4CM
←6CM→

↕6CM
←4CM→

↕10CM
←4CM→

←6CM→
↕2CM

CUT SHAPES FROM FELT AND GLUE IN PLACE TO MAKE VILLAGE AND TREES. MACHINE STITCH DETAILS.

FIX ROUND BASE OF CHRISTMAS TREE

LUREX LOOP

FORM 30CM LUREX PIPE CLEANER INTO HOOP AND TWIST ENDS TOGETHER

SCRAPS

ACCORDION PLEAT 15CM OF 7CM WIDE FOIL CAKE BAND, STAPLE ONE END, FAN OUT AND GLUE TO HOOP

GLUE ON A TWIST OF ANGEL HAIR

Wreath Platters, Christmas Tree Cups, and Candle Napkins

←15 CM→
←25CM→

CUT RING FROM CARD WITH PINKING SHEARS. GLUE TO 23CM PAPER PLATE AND PAINT BERRIES

GLUE ON RIBBON BOW

←18CM→
↕18CM
CUT FROM CARD

CUT CROSS IN CENTRE, DECORATE WITH 14MM STATIONERY DOTS AND GLUE INTO CONE. GLUE SMALL PIECES OF FOAM INSIDE BASE AND ADD MERIT STAR. SQUEEZE FRONT AND BACK AND FIT OVER PAPER CUP. PUSH STRAW THROUGH CROSS

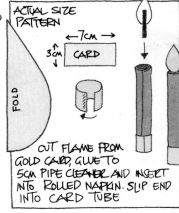

ACTUAL SIZE PATTERN

←7CM→
↕3CM
CARD

FOLD

CUT FLAME FROM GOLD CARD, GLUE TO 5CM PIPE CLEANER AND INSERT INTO ROLLED NAPKIN. SLIP END INTO CARD TUBE

Fancy Dress

Snowman

← 10CM →
NOSE
CUT FROM CARD AND GLUE INTO CONE

↑ 20 CM ↓
HAT SIDES
CUT 1 FROM CARD
← 65CM →

CUT 1 FROM CARD

HAT BRIM
↑ 30 CM ↓

FOLD DOWN 1CM TOP AND BOTTOM AND CUT TABS

TAPE NOSE ON FROM BEHIND

Christmas Tree

← 40CM →
HAT
CUT FROM CARD

STAR
1 SQUARE = 5CM

CUT FROM FOIL CARD

→ 1/8 CHEST + 5CM ←

5CM ↕

UNDERARM TO KNEE + 5CM

SKIRT
CUT 4

FOLD

UNDERARM TO KNEE + 5CM

10CM

← 1/4 CHEST + 5CM →

PLACE BATTERY PACK IN POCKET

Cut knee-length basic jacket pieces from sheeting and thin wadding, and tack pieces together before making up. Elasticate sleeves, and add black button 'coals'. Make basic mask base, draw eyes and add nose, then cover with wadding. Glue hat piece to mask, folding down tabs. Cut out crown from brim to fit, and glue both pieces to tabs.

Sew skirt pieces together, then cover with strips of fringed and gathered crêpe paper. Elasticate top, and insert hoop of boning in hem. Glue hat into cone, then cover with paper fringing and add elastic strap. Sew baubles and bead trimming to costume, and glue foil star to hat. Add extra sparkle with battery operated lights.

Reindeer

Sew antlers together close to edge, leaving base edges open, and stuff with wadding. Fold ear pieces in half and sew to balaclava, together with antlers. Sew tail seam to make a cone, stuff lightly, gather base and sew to back of trousers. Sew satin ribbon round sweater cuffs and trouser hems. Make ribbon harness and trim with bells.

Angel

Join sleeve seams and sew to vest, gathering to fit. Hem cuffs and work 3 rows of shirring 5cm up from hem. Make basic skirt to fit from underarm to floor and trim with star sequins. Draw feather pattern on wings with empty ball point pen, and attach safety pins with sticky tape. Wind pipecleaner and florist's wire halo on to hair band.

Santa's Sack

Join sack pieces, leaving leg holes open in base seam. Neaten raw edges and sew tape round top, 10cm down from edge, with opening at centre front. Thread casing with cord and draw up to fit, padding sack with scrap paper. Cut base from small box which fits head, gift wrap and add elastic strap. Tack toys and boxes over sweater top.

Gingerbread Man

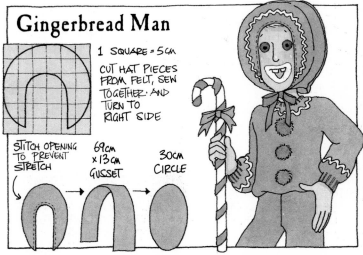

Sew gusset to front and back head pieces and add ribbon ties. Decorate with jumbo ric rac braid and tie on head, padding with strips of wadding. Tack braid on to sweater and trousers, and add wool bobbles. Cover walking stick with white crêpe paper, then wind with red paper and trim with ribbon. Draw round eyes and mouth with face paints.

Food and Drink

Wreath Rolls

CUT HOLE FROM CENTRE OF HALVED ROLLS, THEN SPREAD WITH BUTTER AND FILLING

TINT COLESLAW WITH A FEW DROPS OF GREEN FOOD COLOURING AND SPREAD ON ROLLS

SPRINKLE WITH FINELY CHOPPED RED PEPPER. MAKE BOWS FROM THIN STRIPS OF TINNED PIMENTO

THAT'S THE WREATHS DONE—NOW FOR THE PINECONE!

Cheese Pinecone

BEAT 250g CREAM CHEESE UNTIL SMOOTH, THEN ADD 125g GRATED SHARP CHEDDAR CHEESE

STIR IN 1 TEASPOON FRENCH MUSTARD, 1 TEASPOON CARAWAY SEEDS, 1 TABLESPOON CHOPPED CAPERS, AND SEASONING TO TASTE

PILE ON A PLATE AND SMOOTH INTO CONE SHAPE. SPRINKLE WITH PAPRIKA

PRESS 225g TOASTED BLANCHED ALMONDS INTO CONE AND SERVE WITH SMALL CRACKERS

Yule Logs

MAKE HOLES IN MINI SWISS ROLLS AND PUSH IN SHORT PIECES OF CHOCOLATE FLAKE

HALF COAT GLACÉ CHERRIES WITH MELTED CHOCOLATE, THEN PRESS IN SLIVERS OF CANDIED PEEL AND CURRANTS. PUSH INTO POTATO TO SET

SPREAD LOGS WITH GLACÉ ICING, PRESS IN CHERRY ROBINS AND LEAVE TO SET

I THINK I'LL KEEP MY ROBIN AS A PET!

90

Stained Glass Cookies

CUT BASIC BISCUIT DOUGH WITH LARGE AND SMALL CUTTERS AND PLACE ON TRAYS LINED WITH NON-STICK PARCHMENT

SEPARATE BOILED SWEETS INTO COLOURS. PLACE IN PLASTIC BAGS AND CRUSH FINELY

FILL COOKIE CENTRES WITH POWDERED SWEETS AND BAKE

LEAVE UNTIL CENTRES ARE SET THEN PLACE ON RACKS TO COOL

Festive Cheer

CUT AN ORANGE INTO QUARTERS AND PUSH A CLOVE INTO EACH PIECE

POUR 1 LITRE APPLE JUICE AND 1 LITRE RED GRAPE JUICE INTO ENAMEL SAUCEPAN AND ADD 1 TABLESPOON HONEY

ADD ORANGE PIECES AND A CINNAMON STICK, AND HEAT GENTLY FOR 10 MINUTES

STRAIN INTO CUPS AND DRINK IMMEDIATELY!

Christmas Tree Cake

STIR 4 TABLESPOONS HUNDREDS AND THOUSANDS INTO DOUBLE QUANTITY OF BASIC PARTY CAKE MIXTURE

DIVIDE BETWEEN GREASED FOIL BASINS AND BAKE UNTIL SET IN CENTRE

500ML 150ML

1 LITRE 500ML

COVER ONE 500ML CAKE WITH FONDANT ICING, THEN JOIN CAKES WITH BUTTER ICING AND SPREAD WITH REMAINDER

JELLY STAR

MARK NEEDLES WITH FORK AND DECORATE WITH SWEETS AND SILVER DRAGEES

RIBBON BOW

Games

Santa's Socks

Two teams each have a stocking. Write each player's name on a wrapped empty matchbox and drop into their team's stocking, with 3 plain boxes, then hang them up. The first in line run up and feel for their boxes. When they find them they return to their teams and the next in line take their turn. The first team with all their boxes wins.

My Gift!

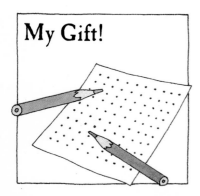

On a piece of paper draw ten rows of ten dots, and give two players a coloured pencil each. The players take turns to draw a horizontal or vertical line, joining two adjacent dots. The person who completes a box with the fourth line draws a bow in the centre. Give a small gift to the player with the most bows at the end of the game.

Trim the Tree

Each team elects a leader who is given a tree cutout. The players must each pick up a gummed shape from a saucer, using only a drinking straw, and take it to their leader, who sticks it on the tree. If the shape is dropped the player must return to start. The winning team is the one with the most decorations on its tree after five minutes.

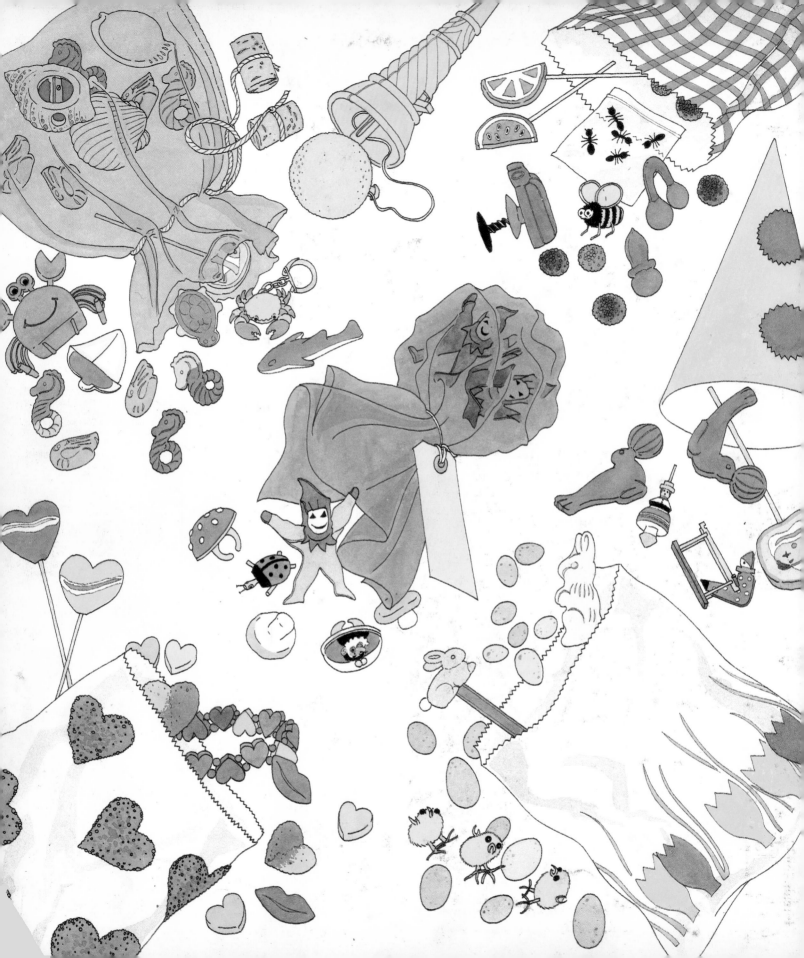